GEEK NERD SUIT

BREAKING DOWN WALLS, UNIFYING TEAMS, AND CREATING CUTTING-EDGE CUSTOMER CENTRICITY

CHUCK
DENSINGER

BROOKE
NIEMIEC

MASON
THELEN

This book was inspired and supported by many people—and it would never have happened without them. First, we want to express boundless appreciation to the Elicit Team for their passion, their brilliance, and their rebellious thinking. We want to thank our clients and partners for literally letting us "into their business"—without the learning we did together, the insights shared in this book would not exist. We're honored and grateful to have worked with every one of you. Thank you to our editors, Jenny Johnson and Nick Leither, for challenging us throughout the writing process, lending your expertise and helping shape this book. For his visual artistry, we sincerely thank our creative director, Jimmy Egeland, who made our words come to life through skillful illustrations and book design. Thank you to our friends and family for supporting us while we carved out many hours of our time to make this book a reality. And the greatest thanks to our spouses—Vicki, Jim, and Danielle—for their encouragement and support through the long hours and months of this project.

So many friends and colleagues share our belief that what the word "customer" means in the modern world must be redefined. Jim "TFJS" Sawyer, Ben Fuqua, Dr. Michael Haydock, Tom Nealon, Bob Jordan, Kevin Krone, Bill Tierney, Ryan Green, Teresa Laraba, Herb Kelleher, Colleen Barrett, Eric Hunter, Andy Laudato, Mariano Dima, Carrie Fisher, Ed Robben, Frank Hamlin, Mike Boylson, Jill Puleri, Bill Hoffman, Mark Putaski, Brian Cuffel, Steve Seabolt, Chris Chapo, Karin Kricorian, Karen Seratti, Fran Phillips, Rebecca Frechette, Steve Harvey, Rich Christensen, Dave Peters, Dave Williams, Rick Porter, Jon Feld, Dr. Alec Johnson, Dr. Bob Eichinger, and Gretchen Twiss—we appreciate your insight, your vision, and your partnership on this path.

TABLE OF CONTENTS

THE DIRTBAG

By now, he's become a living legend. After decades pursuing his passion for the outdoors, his face has taken on the furrowed hills and canyons of the mountains he has climbed his entire life. He has the stout and powerful build of a man who has surfed the most aggressive waves on the planet for five decades. Self-described as a "dirtbag," this barefooted wanderer with no college degree who once lived in a slat-board beach shack in San Blas, Mexico doesn't immediately present as an influential and respected businessman.

Meet Yvon Chouinard, the founder and owner of the American clothing company, Patagonia. Inspired by a Swedenborgian mystic named John Salathé, Chouinard began his business adventures blacksmithing reusable climbing pitons with a portable coal-fired forge in the late 1950s. Surrounded by fellow dirtbags, he sold them handmade pitons and good vibes, surfing the California coast and scaling granite in Yosemite.

Because of his deep understanding of his customers and their needs, demand for his climbing hardware exploded. By the early 1970s, his company, Chouinard Hardware, was the largest supplier of climbing equipment in the U.S. Building on that success, Chouinard and his company began experimenting with clothing and fabrics, ultimately creating what we now know as Patagonia.

Through the 1980s, Patagonia grew at a rapid pace, making *Inc. Magazine's* list of fastest-growing private companies. What had once been a lean company making handmade products for Chouinard's pals was becoming increasingly overweight. In an interview with Guy Raz, Chouinard once said: "There are two kinds of growth, one where you grow stronger and one where you grow fat. And you gotta look out for that growing fat thing."

By the late eighties, Patagonia had grown fat. They were opening retail stores and making new dealer contracts. "We were growing too fast. We were growing fifty percent a year," Chouinard said. But in the summer of 1991, their growth plummeted and they were left with a large inventory of unsold products. They had to scale back and lay off twenty percent of their workforce, and didn't know if they were going to make it or not.

Anyone in business knows that these are the kinds of moments that can make or break a company. In the case of Patagonia, it might be tempting to suggest that they broaden their customer base, decrease the production costs of their clothing, and try to get their products into national big box retailers like Target and Wal-Mart. In short, cheapen their products to serve a mass market, hoping on a prayer and flashy magazine ads that customers will follow and sales will recover.

What did Chouinard and Patagonia do? They returned to their core values. Instead of redefining their customers or broadening their base, Chouinard decided to do the opposite and "…wait for the customer to tell us how much to make." In his 2005 book, *Let My People Go Surfing,* Chouinard writes, "At all levels of corporate activity, we encourage open communications, a collaborative atmosphere, and maximum simplicity, while we simultaneously seek dynamism and innovation." Simply put, Patagonia created a collaborative atmosphere for its employees—from top leaders to the rank-and-file— where they were empowered to listen to the customer.

What Patagonia had learned from their problematic rapid growth was that they had made a critical error in their approach to their customers. What began as an intimate connection had grown clunky, mysterious, big, and detached. The question was, how do you remain customer-centric when your company has grown far beyond the scope of your original dirtbag climbing buddies?

Let's be honest, companies want two primary things: to make money and to please their customers. There are a couple common ways to do this. The first is to trick customers into false desires and a misguided belief that they need your product or service and will suffer through all your ineptitude to get it. The second is to authentically please customers and provide them with products, services, and an experience they value in every interaction they have with your company. If you're interested in the former, stop now, return this book, and go read Machiavelli or *The Wizard of Oz.* If you're interested in the latter, let's take a closer look at Patagonia.

It would be understandable if your takeaway from the Patagonia story was to think, "Here is an example of impeccable leadership from a brilliant man. If I want to succeed, I need to be Yvon Chouinard—or find a Yvon Chouinard and hire that sucker to lead to my company." You wouldn't be completely wrong, either. Chouinard, no doubt, is brilliant, eccentric, and compelling. But what if we told you that his company's continued success isn't really about him? What if we told you that GE's success wasn't about Jack Welch, or Apple's success wasn't about Steve Jobs, or Tesla's success isn't about Elon Musk?

What we can attribute to Yvon Chouinard is, ironically, the opposite of what we so commonly mythologize as leadership and authority. There's no question that Chouinard's vision chartered the course for his company, but it wasn't only Chouinard's ideas that made it successful in the long run. He trusted others and their skillsets to adopt, expand on, and bring his ideas to life. It was his acceptance of his employees' autonomy, and his allowance for collaboration to exist across all of the departments. From the top, Chouinard was taking a step back and creating a collaborative, self-sustaining atmosphere. Don't believe us? Try this: Chouinard took off from the company every June until November, spending his time in Jackson Hole. He would call in to the company three times in five months. "If the warehouse burns down, don't call me. What can I do? You know what to do."

In philosophy and science, there's an idea called "emergence." Often referred to as "bottom-up behavior," emergence is the idea that a larger, collective group or system is capable of complexity beyond any individual part. One ant is pretty dumb. Collectively, however, ants create sophisticated colonies. Bees create intricate hives. Birds create and travel in swarms that seem to move and behave in ways that make it seem they are guided by a single intelligence. A bunch of us individual humans have created immense metropolises, bodies of science, and artistic traditions. And there's no dictator telling any of them or us what to do.

"A lot of companies are top-down management, and it takes a tremendous amount of effort to run those," Chouinard explains. Instead, Patagonia took its mission, values, and knowledge about their customers and spread it out through every department, to every employee, and every part of the business—from the lifetime warranty they wrote for their jackets to their website to their executives to their marketers. In fact, they take great care in only hiring employees who share their passion for customers, knowing that this inner motivation can't be replaced by top-down direction.

The takeaway is simple. There is no isolated team or demagogue that is going to make a company successful. There's no self-help leadership book that is going to turn you into Elon Musk or Yvon Chouinard. There is no hero to save us. But why should that be dispiriting? In fact, isn't it refreshing? It certainly was for Chouinard. Wouldn't it be great if we could create more successful leaders and businesses by relying on the strengths, autonomy, and collaboration of others, trusting that innovation will emerge? In fact, the farther we push that autonomy into our organizations, the closer it gets to our customers. Because it is, in fact, our empowered employees who serve them.

So, all we have to do is get the right people on the team, and empower them to put the customer at the center of everything. Problem is... How?

1

THE ORIGIN STORY

You'd be right if one of the things you took away from the story of Patagonia was to be wary of individual leaders or outside experts who say they have all the answers. On that note, let us introduce ourselves. We are consultants who run a consulting firm called Elicit. But before you chalk us up as some kind of dream team out to change the world, let us tell you where this book came from.

Several yeas ago, we were sitting in the CMO's office at Best Buy, tasked with helping them understand their customers in a changing market. Amazon was famously beginning to turn Best Buy into their showroom, and Best Buy was asking themselves very difficult questions about their future. The CMO, whom we'll call Hadley, was a wiry guy with dark hair and tight sideburns. He had a lightning-quick mind, and eyes that darted around the room as if always on the hunt for something more interesting. We had just completed a behavioral segmentation for the company, and he was impatient for change. "You guys have given us the segments, but my team just doesn't get it."

"What do you mean?" Mason asked. "They seem to understand them perfectly."

"No, I mean they aren't doing anything with them," Hadley said. "They don't know how to use the segments. I'm just getting more pie charts, not more customers."

This was a common complaint and pattern. Helping companies to become more customer-centric often seemed like it should be straightforward. You line up all the customer data. You torture it until it reveals its secrets about your customers, and the positive returns start flowing in, right? On the surface, Hadley seemed to have the right formula: organize the data, analyze it for insights, and act on it. But the company was going about it in the wrong way.

"That's because your analytics team doesn't generate new customers—your merchants, marketers, and stores do, using the technology your IT department manages," Chuck explained. "Why aren't your teams talking with each other?"

Hadley fidgeted, raised his arms in exasperation, and sighed. "Just tell me what I need to do."

Chuck leaned forward. When he glanced over at Mason for some backup, Mason was dialed out, jotting something down in his Moleskine. Chuck stalled, waiting for Mason to return to the conversation. Mason looked up with a curious grin, not saying a word.

"Look," Chuck said to Hadley. "We understand your problem. Give us a few days to think it through, develop an implementation strategy, and meet with you again to present it."

Hadley rolled his eyes, planted his hands on the desk, and said, "Fine." We knew he wasn't assuaged. We were failing at what was supposed to be the easiest part of our job—explaining, in clear detail, our strategy.

Outside, in an adjacent office, Chuck turned to Mason, "What were you doing in there? Writing love letters? Come on. We've got a problem here."

Mason took out his Moleskine, picked up a blue dry erase marker, and headed toward the window. On it he wrote:

GEEK NERD SUIT

We stood in front of the window, staring at those three words. Hadley's problem at that moment was that his teams were just lobbing the ball to one another and failing to communicate. He was getting data and ideas from all of his teams individually, but no collaborative solutions. What Best Buy needed was for its geeks (technologists), nerds (analysts), and suits (strategists) to work together.

Finally, we looked at each other, smiled, and nodded, leaving it on the window as a small artifact of what was to come. And thus, the labels Geek, Nerd, and Suit were born. The ideas had been percolating for some time, but these three words suddenly made it all coalesce. Our minds were racing, ideas flowed, and plans were hatched to help Best Buy. A problem we'd been wrestling with just came together in a big way.

As we walked out of the office, our first thought was, "Let's call Brooke." That afternoon, the three of us talked at length about how this was *the formula*: getting Geeks, Nerds, and Suits aligned was the way to make it work. It was the first of many such sessions, sometimes sitting in conference rooms in preparation for a client meeting, sometimes over a hastily-consumed lunch at an airport, sometimes during "office hours"—our evening work sessions at the hotel bar in which "two bourbon brilliance" worked its magic. The ideas took shape and worked themselves out as we applied them with our clients over the coming months and years.

When we returned to Hadley's office a few days later, we said, "Right now, your Geeks, Nerds, and Suits are working separately, which is paralyzing your ability to make real change. You need them to start cooperating to serve customers instead of creating charts and graphs and overwrought ideas."

It was the first time in weeks that we actually heard Hadley laugh. From that moment on, we restructured the ways in which his teams communicated, shared information, solved problems, and collaborated. Not only did it get Best Buy new customers, it helped them better serve their existing customers, setting the stage for a decade-long, innovative push from a brick-and-mortar big box to a customer-centric behemoth with a unique approach from its competitors, serving customers in stores, online and—in the case of the Geek Squad—in their homes.

We'd realized that what was missing from Best Buy's—and pretty much all of our other clients'—approach to serving their customers better was not vision, desire, or effort. What was missing was true customer centricity, and the right partnership to make it a reality.

Geek Nerd Suit was born in that moment of inspiration, but its roots went back to the times earlier in each of our careers in which we were the ones hiring outside consultants to help our companies become more customer-centric, and we were the ones seeing solution after solution not work. Businesses and the consultants they hired so often failed because they made broad-sweeping decisions about the customer experience and split into isolated teams to address the details of implementation.

From that moment of insight, we fleshed out the ideas, deepened their application, and proved them to ourselves and to our clients time and again in our work—creating collaboration not just in the brainstorm, but in every drop of rain.

2

SHARING OUR SECRETS

Big or small, global or local, we constantly run across companies that are struggling mightily with what we've come to think of as the customer conundrum. These organizations are keen to figure out what their customers really want—and to shift their strategies in order to provide it. But that process often turns out to be much harder than they thought. Many have tried a handful of approaches, only to feel as if they were making zero progress. "I've spent $24 million in the last three years buying all this integrated technology that was supposed to address this, and we're no better off now than we were then," the CIO of an international retailer once told us. Another executive felt buried under all of her great data. "After all this time, I still don't know who my best customers are," she said, bleakly.

If you picked up this book, then you probably already agree that solving this problem matters. By "this problem" we mean three things:

collecting the right customer data, gleaning meaningful insight from that data, and ensuring that this insight directly informs your product, experience, and marketing decisions in ways that make you even more relevant to the people who buy your stuff—and doing so profitably. That, in a nutshell, is customer centricity. It's a serious effort to put deep understanding of customer needs and wants at the center of your strategy and operations. Which makes great sense, given that 100 percent of your revenue equals 100 percent of the spend of your customers. These folks are already driving your business. Customer centricity's promise is that scrutinizing all of those individual customer decisions to interact and ultimately buy from you will lead to powerful new insight into the performance of your business. The intersection of what they want and what you're good at is where value is created. We can improve our top and bottom line while making their experience better along the way.

It sounds simple, right? Get data, build insight, shift strategy. Yet, we're pretty sure we could walk into most Fortune 500 companies in America right now and find a whole bunch of people chugging Red Bull and pulling out their hair while trying to figure out this process. So why are so many companies having so much trouble becoming more customer-centric? In other words, if customer centricity sounds that easy, why is it so hard in practice?

FINDING A FORMULA

The good news: it doesn't need to be that difficult. We spend our days helping businesses understand their customers and infusing that understanding into their decisions and strategies. In the time since we started our business, we've worked with dozens of companies, including industry giants like Southwest Airlines, Intel, Best Buy, HP, Fossil, Sephora, and many others.

Chuck and Mason founded Elicit (and recruited Brooke to join) because we were all obsessed with the same phenomenon. Consumer experiences were clearly changing. Smartphones were taking off, and customers suddenly had the internet in their pockets. The amount of digital data being thrown off by all these new experiences and devices was insane, and accelerating. Companies were deluged by it, and yet they continued to pummel their customers with marketing messages that revealed no knowledge of who these customers were or any sensitivity to what they might care about.

But we knew this would change—that it would have to change. At some point the combination of data and analytics and technology would make it possible for companies to talk to customers like we talk to our close friends. They would know enough about us to know what we care about. That's a sea change—one that we're still in the middle of. And we wanted to be part of bringing it about.

After framing up our formula for transforming a company's customer centricity process—an approach we've helped deliver again and again—we figured it was time to share it.

GEEK NERD SUIT

Remember our definition of customer centricity? It had three parts: get data, build insight, and shift strategy, and each part corresponds to a different part of your business:

- GEEK. Collecting and using the right customer data generally falls on the shoulders of a customer and data technology expert, whom we simply dub the Geek.
- NERD. Gleaning meaningful insight from that data falls to the responsibility of the analytics and research teams, which we

collectively dub the Nerd.

- SUIT. Ensuring that this insight directly informs your brand, product, pricing, customer experience, and marketing decisions to drive your relevancy to customers—well, that's in the hands of the Suit, aka your business and strategy leaders.

Geek, Nerd, and Suit may sound like people, and we suppose they might be. It's more accurate, though, to say that they are all critical functions that can be performed by a combination of individuals or teams. Regardless, the first key to achieving customer centricity is to make sure that each of these functions has the tools and strategies it needs to play its part in the process. The second key is to make sure that all three are working in concert. If they aren't, then it really doesn't matter what else you do or what you may already be doing really well—your customer centricity strategy will be pretty much dead in the water.

WHAT'S INSIDE THIS BOOK

Whatever glitch you are hitting in your quest to become more customer-centric, we've seen it before. Most of these problems arise from a lack of strong partnership across the Geek, Nerd, and Suit functions. We'll explain the traits desired for each function, share what happens when one or more function is weak, and offer solutions for how to get Geek, Nerd, and Suit to collaborate and work together. We will then address the most common challenges we've observed on the path to customer centricity, and include solutions that will help you begin to address those challenges.

IS THIS BOOK FOR YOU?

Here are some very common challenges we face, you have probably faced, and our clients face all the time—challenges that we will directly address in this book:

- Our strategy isn't informed by customer insight
- Our business priorities are confusing, debated, or non-existent
- We want to be customer-centric, but don't know where to start
- We pretty much treat all of our customers the same
- We don't know who our best customers are
- We know what our customers do, but not why they do it
- We don't have a clearly defined "big data" strategy
- Our IT, analytics, and business teams operate in silos
- We don't know what marketing technology to use
- We don't connect customer data across touch points
- We're not effectively managing our marketing dollars
- We aren't testing enough and we learn too slowly
- We aren't curating the end-to-end customer experience
- We don't monitor our business via customer metrics

Recognize yourself in there? You're not alone. The good news is we know these problems can be addressed, and we can help. In our day jobs, we don't just drop off strategy and leave. We teach our clients to do what we do. We share our secrets. We help them build a roadmap for how to become more customer-centric across people, process, technology, data, and analytics. And that's what we hope this book does for you: helps you see the path forward from where you are to where you want and need to be. There is simplicity on the other side of complexity, and we're here to help you start finding it.

So, now that you know a little bit about who we are, the basis for how we developed our methods, and who the Geeks, Nerds, and Suits in your organization are, lets start addressing the challenges and opportunities you have in front of you.

3

GEEK, NERD, SUIT

Imagine for a moment that you just got a call from Susan, SVP of Consumer Products at a company we'll call TFJS Solutions. TFJS Solutions is a multi-national, multi-channel maker and seller of technology solutions that range from consumer electronics to intelligent home technologies to top-secret defense contracts. Susan is a brilliant product manager who has risen to the head of her business unit, and has a warm smile that goes all the way to her eyes. But those eyes also see deeply and don't miss a thing. While she's not one to raise her voice, it's clear when she is displeased. She succeeds through her team, cultivating strong position players, giving them clear direction, and then getting out of the way.

Susan tells you that they are on the brink of a major product launch and she has run into a big issue. The product is behind schedule and is going to be more expensive than planned. Worse, the early read with target customers is not good: this isn't a product they want to buy. She needs help.

What went wrong?

THE AVALON DILEMMA

Susan's team has developed a new consumer product called Avalon, a home monitoring and management system that is something of a marvel. Building on their existing lighting, thermostat, and home appliance technologies, Avalon talks to all of them, managing the consumer's home. Further, it is connected to a smartphone app that becomes the consumer's primary interface. As the homeowner walks from room-to-room, lights automatically come on and off in a gentle fade. Thermostats adjust to preferred temperatures based on sleep and work patterns. The oven can start a roast in time for dinner, and adjust the cooking time if there's terrible traffic on the drive home from the office.

The concept for Avalon arose from brainstorming sessions early on in their customer centricity project. Consumer data, coupled with focus group sessions, indicated it would be a highly successful product. But let's back up for a moment and meet some of Susan's team.

First, we'll introduce Jack. Jack is the head of the IT team—responsible for creating tools, systems, and processes for collecting, storing, and integrating customer data. Jack's a Geek. In the past, he might have looked like a guy who reads too much science fiction, but he's from San Francisco, dresses in flannel, has a beard, and resembles a lumberjack. His team has built a repository of robust customer data over the past few years that is best in class.

Margaret is our Nerd. She wears her hair short and uncomplicated, and peers out at the world through a pair of smart glasses. She is detail-oriented, but also a master synthesizer. She's not just about data—she's about connecting the dots. Her Nerd team not only mines databases for facts and patterns, but also conducts research and focus groups. They are responsible for analyzing all of Jack's data, providing insights, and generating recommendations.

Armed with customer data and research, Margaret's team comes to the conclusion that it is imperative that the Avalon solution be fully-functional from day one, including as many of their envisioned features as possible. There are already down-market products that do parts of what Avalon does. For it to really make a splash, Avalon needs to have it all, and get it right. Margaret verifies this with her knowledge and her data about their customers, takes that insight, and hands it off to Ray.

Ray is our Suit. A quick wit, firm handshake, and Varvatos suit make him the perfect fit for TFJS Solutions' team of strategists. Ray's team must establish and execute the product strategy. Based on the insights from Margaret and her team, Ray's team guides product development as they build out the complex set of features for Avalon, along with the mobile app user experience. They also produced a brilliant strategy around "the fortunate isle" based on the near-paradise of mythological Avalon (which became the product's name). One's home becomes their Avalon, a refuge from the rest of the world, responsive to their every movement and desire for comfort.

They decide to market Avalon to their existing customers, people who have purchased smart appliances, thermostats, and light switches. Their logic is that these customers already show an interest in these types of solutions, and already own components that will integrate with Avalon.

But now, with only 90 days to go until product launch, a number of problems have arisen. Early tests of the product with their target customer have gone poorly. The setup and configuration required to get Avalon working is daunting. Most target customers are are do-it-yourselfers who bought their existing products through mass retailers. But getting Avalon installed and functional is an entirely different level of complexity. Further, most are not interested in adding the additional controls. They may have a smart thermostat already, for instance, but no real need or interest in adding lighting automation.

To compound the problem, product distribution is proving difficult. Avalon includes a device that must be installed and connected to the home wifi. The plan was to sell that device at mass retail stores. The problem is that the big box retailers (e.g., Target and Best Buy) viewed Avalon as a home product for do-it-yourselfers, better suited to home improvement stores like Home Depot and Lowes. But Home Depot and Lowes saw Avalon as a consumer electronics product better sold by Best Buy or Target. And they all feared that the tech support requirements of Avalon would result in high return rates.

Worst of all, the complexity of Avalon is leading to projected launch delays and a higher price than originally planned. Avalon is going to be expensive.

"So, what went wrong and how can we solve it?" Susan asks.

What had gone wrong was this: Jack, Margaret, and Ray had not worked as a team; they'd worked in their functional silos. The data Jack had collected and provided to Margaret was aggregated by product lines and retail outlets. This led to Margaret and her team developing insights based on averages, not individual consumer patterns. On average, customers were interested in all three Avalon features, but individual customers were typically only interested in one function. Further, upon review, there were biases in her focus groups, as the most vocal participants were more affluent and earlier tech adopters than others who were quieter. Finally, there was Ray. His team had created a compelling vision for Avalon from the beginning, and their well-intentioned desire to bring that vision to life had caused them to sway the other teams to their way of thinking. The customer's voice became diminished and distorted.

So, what should they do now? Go deep with the customer, and focus on what they really want.

After re-visiting the data, a new picture emerged. Jack went into transactional archives and got detailed data for Margaret. Margaret re-examined the focus group footage, and looked up data for the most outspoken customers. A pattern was emerging. She fielded some quick new research to confirm this pattern.

The new story was this: there is, in fact, a customer for Avalon! But it's not the DIY-er. It's a more affluent home-owner whose existing TFJS Solutions products were most often bought and installed by contractors on their behalf. The size of this potential customer group was much smaller than envisioned, but these customers were extremely enthusiastic about what Avalon promised to be. And they have large disposable incomes. A higher-priced luxury product was feasible.

When all of this was shared with Ray, he realized his distribution strategy would no longer work. The product vision remained much the same, but the distribution focus needed to shift to wholesale. Marketing efforts targeted not only the consumer they wanted to reach, but designers, builders, remodelers, and contractors who would serve these consumers. Finally, the positioning for Avalon shifted from broad consumer product to flagship product for a revitalized line of advanced home automation systems. Simplified (and less expensive) elements of Avalon would be sold through the home improvement stores. And, in fact, it turned out Home Depot and Lowes did agree to carry Avalon, but targeted to their contractor business, not their consumer business.

Even more important than this final solution was the approach Susan took to getting there. In moments of crisis, all too often the first option is to place a dictator in the situation, the tyrant who controls the Geek team, the Nerd team, and the Suit team. Many companies behave this way, but how is that customer-centric? It only works if the leader happens to have a clear idea of what the customer wants (often this is luck). And it fails to harness the deep skills of your Geeks, Nerds, and Suits, making them mere order-takers. Who wants to work for a company like that?

Instead, Susan brought her leaders together. They worked out their different viewpoints, uses of language, and perspectives on the problem. They bounced their approaches and ideas off of each other. They solved problems together. The beauty of all of this? They each felt empowered, and the voice of the customer led the way.

The dilemma is clear, but we have noticed that companies often— and almost automatically—lean toward the top-down dictator model, sometimes without even considering or identifying the failure of team collaboration. The reason that companies like Patagonia are able to avoid situations like the Avalon example is simple. We know they don't avoid it by plunking Yvon Chouinard down in the middle as the tyrannical magician, working seventy hours a week as a micromanaging maniac. If you want to succeed, and have time to a take a three-month vacation in the process, bring together the Geeks, Nerds, and Suits in the common goal of customer centricity.

IDENTIFYING YOUR GEEK, NERD, AND SUIT

The first step is figuring out who your Jacks, Margarets, and Rays actually are and where they live in your organization. Geek, Nerd, and Suit are functions, and not necessarily three specific individuals. While the number of individuals and the titles of those who might fulfill those functions may differ, the skillsets needed to succeed in those functions do not.

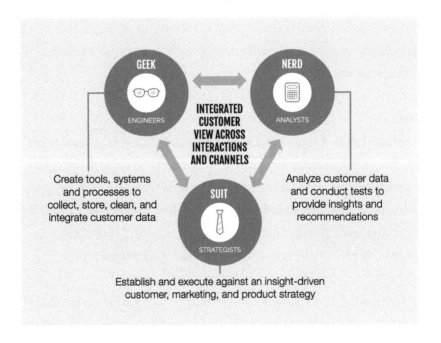

GEEK - systems-oriented IT architect or engineer

NERD - analytically-oriented data miner, modeler, statistician, or researcher

SUIT - customer experience, sales, marketing, or product manager

We chose the terms Geek, Nerd, and Suit to be a little provocative and irreverent. But it's also true that these stereotypes exist for a reason; people do tend to gravitate to work that fits their interests, skills, interpersonal styles, and personality types. There tends not to be a lot of glad-handing and gregarious statisticians, or reserved, deliberative, facts-only marketers. But we do see some. And, increasingly, these atypical traits are being sought out in all fields.

However, there's more to these characters than their stereotypes, and few people fit perfectly into just one of them. Many business-people have experience in multiple disciplines, or have played at the boundaries between these roles. Really, it's their functions in the business that lend themselves to the terms Geek, Nerd, Suit, not their styles or personalities. Let's start by digging into their functions a little deeper.

Geek

This function is responsible for ensuring that the underlying system and data infrastructure is capable of supporting any desired customer communications, interactions, and experiences. The tools need to be implemented, integrated with one another, and enabled to both ingest and use customer data. Not just anybody can make this happen in a way that is smart, efficient, useable, and cost effective.

As we use the term, Geeks are typified by a deep understanding of data and technology and how to use them to make a business more customer-centric. They are systems thinkers, and tend to see the interactions across the whole organization, not just the parts. Data—its capture, management, usage, and flow—is their primary medium. Geeks tend to think in terms of business capabilities—how people, processes, and technology work together to produce business outputs, which could be products, services, or experiences.

The IT department tends to house a lot of Geeks. But not all IT folks are pure Geeks, and there are a lot of Geeks outside of IT departments:

- Business analysts and designers who turn business needs into technical requirements
- Programmers and engineers who build software
- Architects and systems planners who determine how the entire ecosystem of applications and data will interoperate
- Product release managers who ensure new releases are well-orchestrated and well-communicated
- Data and process governance champions who communicate the company's standards for data capture and usage, and enforce those standards
- Specialists in security and privacy

That guy in your department whom everyone goes to when something on their laptop fritzes? Geek. That gal who pops into the manager's office after a marketing meeting and says, "I think the platform needs to do these seven things in order for our new marketing campaign to work." Geek.

Because we are specifically talking about helping companies to become more customer-centric, Geek means something even more specific. It means deep expertise in capturing, managing, and leveraging customer data, and a rich understanding of the plethora of technologies, service providers, and software and hardware companies in the rapidly-growing digital marketing and customer intelligence sector. This landscape is becoming exponentially more complex, as the space has become crowded with thousands of companies that range from consulting firms to database providers to loyalty solutions to web analytics to experience design to, well, you get the picture. Ultimately, it's the Geek's responsibility to make sure the system architecture and standards are set up in a way that they can support what the rest of the business wants to do.

In short, the Geek is there to help gather, organize, and manage customer data in a way that enables insight and action. So, what does it take to be a good Geek? In our experience, the following traits are essential to the success of someone in this role:

- The ability to evaluate a complex network of data and technology
- Subject matter expertise, including awareness of options in the market and an understanding of what will make sense within a specific environment
- A solid understanding of the desired end experience, including what the customers and the business will need in that experience
- The ability to translate direct requirements and inferred functionality into viable alternatives
- An unbiased approach to weighing the pros and cons of possible solutions
- A big picture perspective with an eye for incredibly small details
- An integrated approach to problem solving, and a willingness to ask others for input throughout the design process

Nerd

Nerds also have their own set of large responsibilities. They bear the weight of bringing the customer perspective to life without knowing them personally! *Who are our customers? What do they do? How do they feel about us and our products and services? What matters most to them? What differences exist across the customer base?* Individuals in a Nerd function should have a boundless curiosity about the customer base, and the technical chops to answer whatever questions they come up with. It's the Nerd's job to develop meaningful understanding about customers, and to ensure the organization absorbs that insight.

Nerds have a less obvious or traditional organizational home than Geeks. Most companies have analytic functions spread across departments. Data miners and business intelligence analysts tend to have Geek-like coding skills. Statistical modelers and analysts often have advanced math, statistics, and operations research degrees. Researchers, including ethnographers and focus group facilitators, often have product or marketing backgrounds, and may range from more quantitative to more qualitative in approach and expertise.

The term "data scientist" has become the *de rigueur* Nerd epithet—but only somewhat recently. Before 2005, it occurred rarely in job titles or technical literature, but now is used to entitle almost anyone involved in quantitative work. We consider data science to embody aspects of both Nerd and Geek: the stats and quantitative analysis skills of the Nerd, and the facility with data and programming languages of the Geek.

For those of us who have worked with strong data scientists, we know how exciting it is to have our customer questions answered better than we could have ever imagined. The best Nerds will ask questions in response to being asked for data to learn precisely what they should go analyze—what Margaret failed to do with the Avalon project. They will pursue more than one approach to getting that data, and evaluate the strength of the various options. They will also ask additional questions of the data that are logical follow-ons to the initial question being asked. If you wanted to know how much your best customers spent last year, a good Nerd would also let you know how many times they visited, how much they spent per visit, and what the top five products they purchased were.

Whatever their labels, Nerds are united by trying to understand what makes customers tick. They use data as evidence of customer actions, knowing that each bit of digital data is the result of some interaction or choice. The combination of what customers say (via surveys, interviews, and questionnaires) and what they do (via physical and digital interactions) tells us much about how to relate with and serve them more effectively. Increasingly powerful statistical and algorithmic techniques, coupled with so-called Big Data, can tell us even more. Together, all of these actions have the potential to reveal much about what an individual customer cares about and how she makes decisions—if the Nerd is connecting the dots and providing the insight.

The strongest Nerds will have the following characteristics:

- A deep curiosity about customers and what motivates them
- A love of and desire to explore data
- An analytical approach to problem solving
- The ability to ask good questions
- The ability to translate a business request into a meaningful

data exercise

- A broad knowledge of all available customer data
- A recognition of the limitations of existing data, including any potential biases
- The ability to translate "data speak" into terms that humanize customers

Suit

The Suit is tasked with outlining the customer strategy; spreading the voice of the customer across the business; and wringing value out of the data, technology, and analytics provided by the Geeks and the Nerds. They have to match business objectives to customer needs and create a strategy that maximizes the two. They have to monitor the effectiveness of their decisions and adjust their strategy going forward.

This role is responsible for all of the direct interactions with customers. Suits run stores, manage product lines, provide customer support, and curate customer experiences. They are typically held accountable for the P&L results, and they are subject to two unrelenting masters: the shareholder and the customer. Every company must optimize business value creation for both, and this is generally the job of the Suits.

In most businesses, product and channel strategies drive these interactions. P&Ls, the quarterly and annual scorecards of business performance, reflect the sum of interactions with all customers, typically defined by geographies and lines of business. Ideally, Suits use the data, insights, and capabilities delivered by the Geek and Nerd in order to make better business decisions that generate more value from the business's customer relationships.

Thus, Suits make up the bulk of most consumer-facing organizations, except those few who are heavily driven by technology such as Google, Facebook, or Twitter. Even dotcom giants like Amazon, while heavily tech- and analytics-driven, require extensive Suit activity to manage their supply chain, marketplace, and customer experience execution.

In order to be a good Suit, one must have:

- The ability to create, and gain support for, a compelling vision
- The ability to set micro-customer strategy (for the individual customer) that links to a macro-customer strategy the organization can execute against
- End-to-end knowledge of the current customer experience— and where the moments of truth lie
- A respect for the technology and data underpinnings that enable the desired customer experience
- A solid understanding of data science and research, and the proper uses for each
- KPI setting and accountability
- A pulse on the market, and the ability to balance market factors against company strengths.

HIRING YOUR GEEKS, NERDS, AND SUITS

By now, you should understand the importance of having the right skillset in each of these functions. As you're building out and developing your Geek, Nerd, and Suit functions, keep these tips in mind.

Get Real About Requirements

As marketing, data, and technology start to converge, skill sets for any of these three functions will get more technical across the board. While you can't expect everyone to come in to your business knowing everything, use the characteristic summaries for each function above to ensure you're hiring folks who will excel in that particular role. It's easier to train a technical skill than to train a particular mindset.

Look for Hybrids

When you're hiring for one role, keep an eye out for candidates who have a blended background in more than one function. For example, Data Scientists with some coding background will deliver better, faster results than those who don't. Besides the obvious benefit of hiring someone who can do more than one thing, an important benefit of a diverse background is that they will understand the language of their Geek, Nerd, and Suit counterparts and improve your cross-functional team relationships.

Conduct Cross-Functional Interviews

Knowing that your team will be stronger if team members are skilled at building relationships across the entire Geek-Nerd-Suit spectrum, invite a counterpart from the other two functions to interview high potential candidates. It's as important to hire someone who can bridge these roles as it is to hire someone who meets the technical requirements of their specific role.

Assuming you have filled each of the roles appropriately, however, doesn't guarantee your success. Jack, Margaret, and Ray were each proficient in their functions. The next obstacle to address is the challenge of getting Geeks, Nerds, and Suits to operate together effectively. But how do you do that when they each view the world so differently?

4

GEEK + NERD + SUIT

A few years ago we had a memorable lunch with the CMO of a $20 billion company. With her hair in a neat side part, and a permanent smile in her eyes, Karen greeted us in an executive dining room with red curtains, plush carpet, and a wait staff donning white gloves. The meal was delicious, but Karen strangely kept cutting her food into smaller and smaller pieces. Meticulously and elegantly, she sliced green beans and shallots, but never seemed to take a bite. Though conversing, she kept glancing at us nervously, her plate resembling a bunch of disconnected Legos.

A pale look on Karen's face suggested that either she'd taken a bad bite or something big was bothering her. Turns out, it wasn't the food.

Karen had a problem. Her company was collecting tons of data on its customers. There was, she knew, tremendous value hidden within that jumble—great information they could use to better understand and serve customers in ways that were real, relatable, and personal, involving not a shred of artifice or guesswork. But she had no clue how to get at this information, or exactly what to do with it once she did.

Finally, she put down her knife and fork. "I know so much about 50 million people," Karen confessed. "And I have no idea where to start."

Now, the first impulse might be to suggest that they hire an outside analytics team who would roll up their sleeves, dig in, and create ten crystal clear take away messages from those 50 million people and their data that would make the company better at serving their customers.

We can all see the seduction of that solution. Throw some money at it and let the experts do their thing, right? The problem is, that approach simplifies the challenge, relies on some serious magical thinking, and disenfranchises your own employees.

Let's pretend, for a moment, that Jack, Margaret, and Ray are on the job. Ray, our representative Suit, advises Jack, our Geek, based on his knowledge of company strategy, about what data he should home in on and collect. Margaret, our Nerd, also conveys to Jack the kind of data, based on Ray's strategy, that she will need in order to connect that data with the strategy. And Jack will let both Margaret and Ray know that, while he has a lot of data, he might need to collect some better data in one or two areas if they really want to get valuable insight and create smart strategy.

Karen didn't need an outside analytics team, even though her problem had a lot to do with analytics and insight. If Karen needed external support at all, it would be for a team that could actually create meaningful connections and collaborations within her own business, activating her own employees. That's where we started. We established interdependence between Karen's Geeks, Nerds, and Suits.

THE FUNCTIONAL COMPLEXITIES

By now it should be obvious that the Geek, Nerd, and Suit need to work together. How can a Suit deliver new products and experiences without the data and technology of the Geek, and the analytics and insight of the Nerd? How can the Geek build the right commerce, customer service, and marketing systems for the organization without the business guidance of the Suit, or the Nerd's deep understanding of which data are most critical to understanding customers? How can the Nerd provide meaningful insight without data that is reliably captured and structured by the Geek, or the Suit's guidance as to which customer questions are most critical to the business?

In fact, these roles do co-exist and interact in most organizations. IT departments serve their business constituents. Analytics and business intelligence teams exist within functional departments. Yet, the signs of Geek, Nerd, and Suit not working well together can be seen almost everywhere. Here are some common warning signs.

- "My IT department is so slow, and so expensive, I've just started working directly with an outside firm who can give me what I need."
- "My analytics team just doesn't get it—I keep getting back

spreadsheets and charts that don't actually answer my question."

- "We'd like to give Marketing what they need, but they can't clearly articulate anything. So, we've been building them a new system based on what *we* think they really need."
- "Our data is such a mess, we can't get a consistent answer to a simple question. Every team has different numbers."
- "Our web analytics partner, loyalty provider, and media agency all claim to be able to do the same thing: help us drive better conversion. Who do I believe?"
- "We have this amazing new predictive model that is 85% reliable, but we haven't made a single extra dollar using it."
- "I have such an incredible amount of interaction data about my customers, but I still don't feel smarter about how to serve them."

Or, worse yet, how about these statements?

- "Every time I call your company, the person on the phone acts like they know nothing about me."
- "Your emails never say anything interesting to me."
- "Why don't you offer loyalty benefits I really care about?"
- "You keep showing me the same products that I'm not interested in."
- "I bought that two months ago; why are you still showing me online ads about it?"
- "I've fixed the spelling of my name twice in your system, and it's still using the wrong one."
- "Unsubscribe."

Every one of these statements—whether made by an employee

within a company, or by one of its customers—arises from some form of Geek, Nerd, and Suit not working together effectively. If a moment ago it seemed so obvious that they should do so, then why are these situations so prevalent?

For starters, the nature of the work of these various roles tends to create different perspectives, unique ways of seeing the world, and a host of assumptions heaped onto them by others.

Suits feel the pressure of performing. They are measured monthly or quarterly on financial results. They watch daily or even hourly business performance metrics. They answer to customers who have complaints. They are compared to the competition—by both customers and shareholders. They tend to be action-oriented, outward-focused, and are used to making decisions with incomplete information, despite others often assuming they know it all. Because of this, they tend to be motivated by results, which can range from seeing the smile on a customer's face, to making a sale, to reporting improved profits.

Nerds swim in seas of data, teasing meaning from the Big Data ocean of observations and actions, looking for patterns, and making predictions. They've learned about statistical significance, confidence factors, and variance. They've been burned by bad data, sampling error, and outliers. They are often deliberative, technically precise, and never quite happy with their results. Because of this, Nerds tend to be motivated by solving a problem, uncovering a new insight, or finding a quantitative way to resolve a debate about the business, or about customers. The best Nerds love telling a story revealed by data, and seeing the lights go on in the eyes of their audience.

Geeks live in a complex world of interrelated software, hardware, networks, data, and flows of information. They are systems thinkers, and tend to see broad patterns of interaction. They build capabilities that enable the business to run, and navigate the increasingly complex landscape of options to solve these challenges. All too often, corporate IT departments are their habitats, and these poor Geeks face increasing business demands they find difficult to meet. Sadly, the best they can hope for is avoiding attention (meaning nothing is broken). Some Geeks are the heroes in tech-oriented firms, where engineers and developers rule the roost. Whichever it may be, the best Geeks are motivated by solution elegance. Whether it's a block of code or a large-scale systems implementation, Geeks take joy in the beauty of finding that perfect answer to the challenge, obvious in hindsight, simple yet complete.

The challenge that can arise naturally from these necessarily different skill sets is that all too often, Geek, Nerd, and Suit do not really speak each other's languages. As we can see by the differences in how they're motivated, they often view the world differently, and may be solving for different things when facing a business challenge. They may also have misaligned priorities and views about what the organization needs. For instance, the Suits may be demanding a quick answer to an urgent issue; the Nerds may be anxious about getting the data right; and the Geeks may be contemplating the long-term consequences of a short-term "patch."

While each may have a similar desire to advance the organization, they may not have the skills needed to partner with each other. At best, they may simply not have enough familiarity with the other's technical language to understand one another; at worst, they may be in open conflict because of misalignment.

IS ONE GOOD ENOUGH?

Geek Only: Amazing but Lonely Technology

We've worked with many organizations that were established by, and are still run by, technologists and engineers. However, if the Geek operates independently for too long, you can end up with amazing systems that have no true insight about customers—rendering them inferior or even useless—and no ability for business users to understand and act on customer insight across the entire customer journey. We can't tell you how many companies we have seen invest in best-in-class tools, or build extensive application systems, only to have their terabytes of data sitting disconnected and unusable in service of customers.

Nerd Only: Questionable Data without Results

A Nerd operating independently will face two challenges. The first is that they will have limited access to questionable customer data, making the results of their analysis also questionable. Why? Because if the Geek hasn't done their job, the data is likely to be incomplete, inaccurate, or unlinkable. Second, even if the Nerd works around the lack of transactional data by conducting some in-depth customer research, the insight generated won't have a sponsor in the business who can adjust decision-making accordingly.

Suit Only: Unfulfilled Dreams

Our experience has included encounters with a number of business leaders who face this situation. They know exactly what they want to do, but they don't have the technology to execute any of it or the analytics to justify investing in any of it. It's incredibly frustrating to those leaders, and often ends with their departure from the organization. At best, heuristics take over, and Suits operate under the assumption of long-held beliefs and rules of thumb.

HOW ABOUT TWO?

Geek + Nerd: Solid Models on the Shelf
This combo will get you the ability to capture data, and the ability to analyze that data. However, you'll lack the partner to actually leverage anything you've built, so your amazing data and insight will go exactly nowhere.

Nerd + Suit: Active Decision-Making With Bad/No Data
In this situation, the Suit and Nerd are in much the same spot as above. The Nerd has poor data to work with, only now with a frustrated Suit asking them for answers. The Suit has a Nerd partner, but no ability to get reliable insights, or to act on the insights they do have.

Geek + Suit: Active Decision-Making With Raw Data
This combination is fairly common. Organizations without a strong Nerd function end up with business leaders who have to make decisions based on giant lumps of raw information. This combo can result in some pretty irrational decision-making.

THE FORMULA FOR SUCCESS

When we say that Geek + Nerd + Suit is a "formula," we don't mean to imply that there is a one-size-fits-all solution to your customer centricity problems. Although the combined effort of Geek, Nerd, and Suit is the key, the solutions that come from that formula are never the same. All companies operate in different environments. Your customer base is yours and yours alone, because your unique value proposition (UVP) if truly unique, is unlike any other. We've

found that there are some universal principles in becoming customer-centric, but each organization's journey is different, and the
solutions are bespoke, not off-the-shelf.

To add to the confusion, the world is flooded with products, technologies, and firms claiming to have a single-point solution to a
problem that cannot be solved that way. Announce that you don't
know much about the top 25 percent of your best customers, and
you will hear any number of the following: "If you buy these two
pieces of hardware and software, everything will just work automatically." Or, "Our analysts will build you a model that will address all
of your customer challenges." Or, "You don't need any new data or
insight, you just need to make better decisions."

If we've learned one thing, it's that none of these disciplines alone
will ever solve for the future that is already on its way. In fact, these
roles are already starting to converge across the industry.

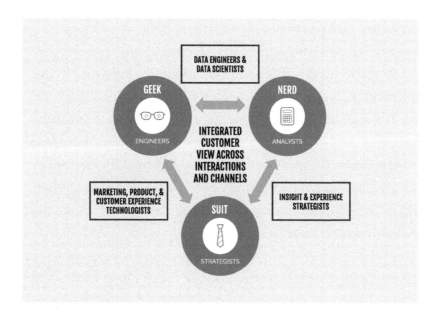

You may already be seeing some of these hybrid roles across your organization:

- Lean Six Sigma Black Belts = Geek + Nerd
- Marketing Technologists = Suit + Geek
- Financial Planning and Analysis Managers = Nerd + Suit
- Tableau Dashboard Builders = Geek + Nerd
- Website Managers = Suit + Geek
- Market Research Strategists = Nerd + Suit

Time and again, we've seen organizations that were previously stuck take giant leaps forward when they get these three functions working in harmony. This is hard work, and is the subject of the rest of this book. Geeks, Nerds, and Suits need to learn one another's language, understand each other's different motivations, and, critically, value the gifts and abilities of the others. But the payoff can be transformational: truly integrated and compelling customer experiences, tailored to customer differences, informed by deep insight, and driving business results through the roof.

A customer centricity transformation can be a long journey. That lunch with Karen was the start of a four-year relationship we had with her and her company. Along the way, there were numerous challenges, and her team did end up needing some Geek, Nerd, and Suit help from us in specific areas. But throughout it all, the primary focus was bringing their internal Geeks, Nerds, and Suits together, helping them to speak a common language, and building the skills needed to achieve their vision.

The remaining chapters explore many of the common road blocks we've encountered, and some Geek + Nerd + Suit approaches to addressing them.

5

PRACTICE DATING YOUR CUSTOMERS

One of our favorite clients—we'll call her Rose—works for a retailer who has long asked their customers to share some of their hobbies and interests. Things like:

- Fine art
- Scrapbooking
- Travel
- Fashion
- Animals
- Collectibles
- Technology
- Literature
- Exotic cuisine

"Rose," we said, "if you were going on a blind date, would you start by handing the person you're just meeting a sheet with this list, and ask them to check the boxes that appeal to them?"

"Well, no, but I would probably ask them their interests in the course of conversation."

"From a checklist?"

"Of course not!"

"And after hearing that they're passionate about travel, would you ignore that comment and change the subject to scrapbooking?"

"OK," she said, rolling her eyes. "I get it!"

It sounds silly to ask. Yet this is exactly what a lot of organizations do when they collect data about their customers. First, they ask for information that, frankly, isn't relevant to their products or services. Second, they don't use it effectively in how they talk to and relate with that customer.

Getting to know someone takes time. You build trust. You integrate what you're learning into your conversations. There's give and take. It's organic.

Most companies know that they need to create relationships with new customers quickly, and they forget the social protocols that accompany relationship building. They are so focused on snagging new customers—and getting them to spend money—that they ask upfront for every bit of information they can think of, whether it is relevant or not. Like desperate singles, they make the classic mistake of calling too soon after the first date, compounding the problem by asking their love interest, "By the way, how many kids do you want after we get married?" It's too much for a first interaction—especially when the customer being blitzed is still making up his or her mind about the company and its products or services. Often, it's more of a commitment than most new customers are willing to make. At best, they ignore the request and go on with their business. At worst, they find the company a little too pushy and reject the proposal.

No matter how craftily a company disguises its efforts to learn everything about a customer before they even *are* a customer, that customer can smell the desperation. See if you can smell it, too:

- Websites that make you provide an email address or register for an account before you can see any content
- Aggressive attempts to get you to join a loyalty program immediately, even if you haven't shown any interest or made a purchase
- Display ads that, once clicked—even by accident—stalk you for at least a month
- Account profiles that ask you for a laundry list of personal information, including hobbies or interests that have no relevance to the company's products or services
- The endless email barrage trying to win you back after an initial interaction, reminding you of an abandoned cart, or worst of all, just pelting you with generic marketing messages

Which brings us back to Rose. Her company was making an honest attempt to learn more about their customers, but it was a misguided one. The data collected from this profile information was not in use, and for good reason—there was no organic and meaningful way to incorporate that random, unrelated data into personalized communications or merchandising about the products they sold. Leveraging our principle of only asking for what you plan to use, we told Rose that they should stop collecting this data. She agreed.

But that wasn't the end of it. Despite her CRM leadership role, there was still resistance to the idea, in part because there was a fear that it would turn out to be useful some day in the future. To demonstrate that it might be a stretch to put this data into use, we created the following hypothetical campaign to demonstrate what it could look like if they did incorporate this data into their marketing communications.

In this one image that we playfully dubbed "Tech Horse," we leveraged each item in the list of customer hobbies. Admittedly, we had a little fun, perhaps even at Rose's expense, but she posted this on her office wall, and used it in select PowerPoint presentations. Finally, her colleagues started to come around. The hobby and interest questions were slated for removal in the next site update.

So how do you court new customers while avoiding the pitfalls of this overzealous first-date syndrome? By practicing a little restraint—and pacing yourself through the getting-to-know-you process.

We advocate progressive data capture. The idea is to ask customers the most important things first—and, even better, just one piece at a time, in a context in which it makes sense. At each interaction, you set the simple goal of asking the "next best question"—or what you naturally need to know next to continue to build the relationship with the customer. Keep in mind that what you can ask depends on the status of your relationship with them; if they've just made their first purchase, thank them, and treat them as a new customer, not someone who's interacted with your brand for years. The questions must be relevant, useful, and within the context of the current interaction.

In normal human interaction, when you meet someone you might want to date, the most natural first question to ask would be the other person's name. This basic rule holds true for initial face-to-face customer interactions as well, whenever employees want to demonstrate interest in a particular customer. If the customer feels welcome and acknowledged, then the hope is they will feel inspired to come back for a second visit.

But in the digital world, name is *not* always the most natural or important piece of information to capture. So what is? Well, follow the same rule, and keep it natural. Only gather, or ask for, what is necessary given the customer's level of interest and commitment. Build gradually. The following table is illustrative of what might be gathered, and for what purpose, at various stages of engagement:

CUSTOMER ACTION	SAMPLE DATA GATHERED	SAMPLE USES
First visit to website	Cookie ID	Digital tracking, retargeting, dynamic content for return visit
First visit to store	Introduce self, ask for name	Associate rapport building
First purchase	Payment info, shipping address (if online)	Store order history; offer loyalty program enrollment
Agrees to enroll in loyalty program	Name, birthdate, email address, permission to share offers and email	Periodic loyalty newsletters, targeted offers, birthday gift
Second purchase	Ask for email address if we don't have it yet	Refine offers accordingly, offer loyalty program enrollment if still not in
First loyalty redemption	Track redemption details	Use to refine loyalty communications, offers
Writes a product review	Take note that it happened!	Thank them, flag them for inclusion in customer panel/forum

Start with some form of contact information that can serve as a pervasive customer identifier across multiple channels, for future interactions, like an email address. But don't force questions on someone just arriving to your site. Let them browse and enjoy the content they came for. Maybe make a purchase. Then, at an appropriate time in the experience, you might ask, "We hope you enjoyed [insert content name]. May we stay in touch with you about content like this?" Experiment with different approaches, remembering that what works for some types of customers may not work for others.

Over time, in order to communicate relevantly and personally, you'll want to collect all of the following information. Develop a customer experience strategy that enables you to do so organically. Some of these you'll ask, some you'll just observe and remember:

- First and last name
- Mailing address
- Phone number
- Product preferences
- Communication preferences
- Demographics
- Birthday
- Payment information
- Preferred store/channel
- Preferred mobile features and usage
- Cadence of marketing and relationship messages
- Price sensitivity and affinity for deals, coupons, and sales
- Missions they come to you for—and those they don't

Start by focusing on data that will make the customer experience better, and on that topic, only ask for information that you plan to use right away. Carefully watch which asks are received well, and which result in customers backing away. Quickly adjust to what is working and what is not.

A few previous big lessons apply here too. First, remember what customers tell you! If they do tell you their name, email address, or anything else, remember it, and act like you remember it. If James tells you he goes by Jimmy, you'd better start calling him that. Second, pay attention to other things your customers are telling you based on *what they do*. For instance, if you email them and they don't respond, but they do react to in-app messages or content, then remember that and use it. If they're interested in one product category, but not another, then remember that and act accordingly.

The good news is that some companies are already effectively building customer knowledge and relationships over time, and we can learn from them. LinkedIn, for example, uses the progressive profiling concept incredibly well. Users can complete their LinkedIn profile at their own pace, and will be prompted by a question every now and then to help strengthen their profile. Further, the company uses a scoring system to tell users how complete their profile is, which acts as a call to action encouraging them to provide more info.

Similarly, HomeAway gives homeowners looking to rent their properties the chance to complete their listing details over time. Like LinkedIn, they also track listing completeness and provide a score that indicates the strength/desirability of a property. When customers haven't recently logged into their account, an email prompts them as a reminder.

What both of these companies have gotten right is giving customers the flexibility to provide information on their schedule, and finding ways to motivate them to add more information over time. Moreover, these companies are not simply collecting data to profile their customers for the benefit of their business. Instead, they use it to help boost customer experience and engagement, in this case through improved professional networks or property rentals.

In order to win at the dating game, first and foremost, you need a customer experience strategy built on the concept of progressive data capture, in which the customer wants to share information with you because it makes their experience better. You also need a strong customer data capture process supported by good technology, great analysis, and the right kind of testing. Not only do you need to date your customers, your Geeks, Nerds, and Suits need to do some dating, too.

6

NICE TO MEET YOU AGAIN, AGAIN

Let's face it: we've all had customer support interactions that have left us feeling less than cared for. See if this one feels familiar. You're scheduled to fly from Dallas to San Francisco at 6pm but you want to leave sooner. So you call your favorite airline for assistance. Your request isn't difficult—checking on the possibility of going standby on an earlier flight. At most, it might take a few minutes to determine whether that's feasible.

Except it takes way longer than that.

After dialing the airline, you're greeted by a voice recognition system with questionable listening skills. Luckily, the system recognizes your phone number. *Great,* you think. *It knows who I am.* Yet somehow the system doesn't seem to have access to your reservation or, for that matter, anything else about you. So it starts asking for all sorts of basic information about your flight: departure date, destination, etc. You do your best diction-coach impersonation—at an inappropriately loud volume—to ensure that the system understands your answers, but a few of them take several tries.

After a series of garbled videogame noises, more button pushing, and more diction-coach impersonating, you feel you must be nearly through the gauntlet. But then—six minutes into the call—the automated voice finally asks you why you are calling. More button pushing and garbling ensue. Eventually you're told that you can wait approximately eight minutes for an agent or have the next available one call you back. *That's a nice gesture,* you think—until, upon opting for #2, the voice prompts you to reenter your phone number, the same one it automatically recognized when you first called.

Fifteen minutes later, your phone rings. You battle your way through another button pushing exercise, jabbing the keys a bit harder than necessary. Finally, you hear a live voice. The agent asks you to provide your flight information all over again. Then she tells you in about 30 seconds that standby is not available. It might have been quicker to drive to the airport and ask there. Or just walk to San Francisco instead.

Because airlines are notorious for this sort of customer experience, we call it "the airline effect." It shouldn't happen—not to loyal customers, and not to new ones either. Forcing customers to run through an obstacle course of automated questions is bad enough. But having them do that when they know full well that somewhere in its system, the company already knows everything about them— reservations, preferences, what they might need, etc.—well, let's just say it does not leave them feeling valued. In fact, it can make them feel like going elsewhere.

So why does this happen? Why do some companies that gather all this rich data about individual customers sometimes seem to know nothing about them at all? Simply put: because their technology and data systems aren't integrated into the customer experience. In other words, they store the data, but don't or can't use that data—at least not when they're interacting with customers. As a result, those customers can feel like they're constantly reintroducing themselves to nobody. To wit:

- A customer updates her mailing address at a physical store location, but continues to receive credit card statements at her old address.
- An airline diligently tracks the credit card miles its customers earn, but does not track how good (or bad) their experiences were.
- A retailer continues to send a customer emails about men's clothing, even though that customer (a woman) has only ever purchased women's clothing.
- Upon checking into a hotel that he visits weekly, a business traveler is greeted with the question, "Is this your first time staying with us?"
- After completing an online checkout as a guest, a shopper is prompted to create a permanent profile to make future ordering easier. When the shopper clicks that option, she is taken to a web form that doesn't remember the info she just filled in when she placed her order.

We have one colleague who has been trying to change his name in a retailer's system for roughly a year. No matter how many times or how many ways he attempts to change it, within a month he is back to receiving communications as "LASTNAME MIDDLENAME" instead of "FIRSTNAME LASTNAME." Think he feels warm and fuzzy about shopping with them? Take it from us: he doesn't.

Each time a company fails to remember something important about a customer, it chips away at the relationship they're trying so hard to build. The truth is that customers don't offer their information as a gift to you. In fact, it's not for *you* at all. It's for you to use to make *them* feel seen, heard, and remembered. In all channels. Every time.

There are examples of companies out there that are getting this right. If you tell Sephora that you have frizzy hair, you will get targeted emails offering you the best taming solutions. If you make a purchase on Amazon, they will recommend products based both on your specific purchase history as well as the purchase history of others who bought what you bought. And, to offer a positive counter-example to the airline interaction at the beginning of the chapter, American Airlines will remember your searches and send you emails with flexible pricing options to your desired location.

Luckily, successfully integrating customer data and customer experience is often simpler than it seems. But it requires action by all three players: the Geek (🄖), the Nerd (🄝), *and* the Suit(🅂).

🄖 🅂 CREATE A SIMPLE WAY TO IDENTIFY YOUR CUSTOMERS

There are lots of ways to identify your customers, but things can get messy if you allow too many to coexist at once. It is much easier to manage a single universal customer identifier—preferably one your customers can actually remember, such as their email address or mobile phone number. A loyalty account number can also work, but give the customer an easy way to self-identify if they can't remember it. Once the identifier is selected, create business rules to link and match customer data to that single identifier in order to avoid the airline effect. In fact, there are many companies that will happily do this for you.

❻ ❺ REMEMBER YOUR CUSTOMERS

As a customer, when you experience the airline effect, the implicit message the company is sending you is that they don't care enough about you to consider your experience. As a business, invest in the infrastructure to capture the data your customers are willing to give you, at any point of interaction. This ranges from the more obvious interactions (such as online account creation) to the more personal (such as interacting with a store employee). Every interaction with a customer is a chance to learn more about who they are and what they care about. But you'd better have a way to remember the things they think are important enough to share. It's best to go slow and get good at the basics before trying to achieve more sophisticated relationship management, like remembering details of conversations between employees and customers.

❶ ❺ MODEL WHAT MATTERS

There are hundreds (even thousands) of things you could learn about your customers. While it's a nice thought to try to capture and track everything, the reality is that some subset of those bits of information really drives differences in behavior. The trick lies in experimentation to see what works. If you are a retailer collecting product preferences and interests, test sending targeted emails to see if it makes a difference. If it doesn't, get rid of it. And it bears repeating: it's not about what matters to you. It's about what matters to your customers.

❻ ❺ ONLY ASK FOR WHAT YOU PLAN TO USE

Once you narrow down the list of what matters, stop asking for information that doesn't. With the increasing focus on capture of personal information, customers are becoming wary of sharing data that they don't think will be used to make their experience better. Don't ask for your customer's communication preferences if you don't have the intent (and the ability) to take them into consideration when you interact with them in the future.

🄝 🅂 KNOW WHEN TO BE IMPLICIT

If a customer tells you something about their preferences, you need to remember it—and you need to *use* it as well. But much of the time customers won't tell you what you really want to know. In that case, you'll need to infer from their behavior what you haven't had a chance to ask them directly. For example, if a customer only browses or purchases your dog treats, it's unlikely they'll be interested in your fabulous discounts on treadmills for mice. Try to use the indirect clues your customers are leaving for you with how they interact with you.

🄝 🅂 DON'T SELL SNAKE OIL

There is something quite irritating about companies that only talk about what matters to them rather than what matters to the customer. If a customer always turns down your offer to add an extended warranty to their electronics purchase, you'd both be better served if you offered them something else that they might truly value. Forced upsells to meet sales quotas smell of just that, and today's customers recognize it and resent it. Instead, offer alternatives that might be of use to the customer based on their behavior and observed needs. For example, an online greeting card retailer could offer extras that add convenience to a customer's purchase, such as preprinted return labels or a fully automated shipping option.

❻ ❽ DON'T FORGET THE BAD

Tracking product failures, service interruptions, and complaints at the customer level are often more important than tracking the good stuff. Imagine if an airline customer who experienced a delayed flight received a personal communication from a service representative upon their return. Or, even better, if the flight attendant on their next flight offered them a complimentary cocktail to make up for it. Remembering the bad can enable excellent service recovery, which in turn can drive greater loyalty.

THE TAKEAWAY

In human relationships, we're expected to recognize someone we've met before. If we know them well, then we're on the hook to remember the personal stuff they've told us about themselves, too. Imagine sending a "happy anniversary" card to a close friend…who got divorced three years ago. Disaster, right? Well, that's the sort of gaffe that companies that don't tie stored data to real interactions commit all the time. If a business really wants to make their customers feel seen, heard, and remembered—in other words, to create engaged customer relationships—then they need to follow these basic principles of human interaction:

- Create a single (and simple) way to uniquely identify them.
- Invest in the technology to capture customer data—and tie all of that information to a known customer at each touchpoint.
- Track both the successes (purchases) and the failures (service interruptions) experienced by each customer to make sure you have a complete view of the customer relationship.
- Infer customer preferences through their behavior.
- Experiment by sending personalized communications with the data you have and let go of anything that doesn't work.

7

I CAN'T PROVE VALUE WITHOUT INVESTING FIRST

It was one of our first meetings with Leo, the CMO of major con-sumer retail chain—a big one, with thousands of stores worldwide. After walking us through the company's current strategic plan, Leo leaned back in his chair, took off his glasses, and sighed. Then he made a confession that sounded remarkably like the one we'd heard from Hadley. Actually, we hear some version of this all the time. "I know there is value locked up in our customer data," he said. "But I have no idea how much it's worth."

For years, the company had been collecting data on one of the most elusive yet desirable cross-sections in the market: 18- to 24-year-old males. In fact, they *owned* that market—one that most retailers can't get to at all. But the troves of data they'd been collecting lived all over the company, each bit disconnected from the rest. And none of it was being used to help the company better understand this incredibly valuable consumer set. Instead, it was just sitting there, gathering electronic dust, and aging its way into complete irrelevance.

In the meantime, market forces were beginning to change the fundamentals of the company's business model. The landscape had become more competitive, and those valuable 18- to 24-year-olds that had historically driven the company's success were beginning to be wooed elsewhere.

Leo fundamentally believed that the company's repository of customer data held the key to ever greater customer engagement—and, ultimately, even greater company profits. He badly wanted to invest in the infrastructure needed to turn that data into insight, including getting all of the data in one place, upgrading the company's CRM platform, and building an integrated customer data warehouse. But without any way to prove his theory upfront, he was unable to secure the funding he needed to build a better system. No wonder he felt defeated.

You can imagine Leo's frustration at being asked to prove the value of what he wanted to implement without actually implementing it. "What do I do?" he said to us, throwing up his arms. "Create a virtual world to test it out just to prove it will work in our world?" The company's leaders were unwilling to make the investment without concrete evidence that the investment would be worth it. We see this in many companies, so how should a leader handle this catch-22?

In the case of Leo, he needed a new customer data warehouse that would bring his data together so he could actually use it and analyze it. But if he had needed, say, to implement a new loyalty program, develop a better campaign management tool, or build a master data management system, the company's leaders probably would have reacted the same way. All of these technologies require fairly significant capital investments. And, all of them come with big promises that executives have heard before and are hesitant to trust.

Unfortunately, we see many companies struggle to make investments at the right time. When things are working well, there isn't a perceived need to invest in infrastructure. Then, by the time business performance starts to sink, it's too difficult to get the funding needed to turn things around.

Why is this so common? First, because humans are risk averse—and rightfully so. Smart leaders need a healthy sense of caution so they avoid wasting money. Further, there are tons of examples of *huge* investments in this space that didn't ultimately pan out. At some point, most of these leaders have been sold technologies or services billed as black-box solutions that could effortlessly address their most pressing business challenges—but didn't. So it's no surprise that leaders are wary of investments that don't come with up-front proof points or money-back guarantees. Especially since none of these systems are necessarily easy or cheap to implement.

The number of possible tools, systems, and interfaces that manage customer data and interactions is astounding. Moreover, even if you are able to loosely diagram your current system architecture, chances are there are numerous customizations that live only within the minds of a few employees, some of whom may no longer work for your organization. These networked, customized systems make it extremely difficult to tackle just one subcomponent at a time, especially when the objective is to get customer data to move freely and accurately through the entire system. This complexity is yet another reason why leaders are so hesitant to invest in system enhancements.

Successful investments tend to be protected within a company's walls to sequester their business secrets, so best practices are hard to discover. The net result is that there is much caution in this space. Which, in turn, helps fuel the "prove it" problem that Leo faced—even though everyone knows that it's pretty hard to prove the value of something you've never tried. Their demand for proof isn't going to change. So we need to get better at showing how these investments lead directly to actions that have positive business results.

Investments also get sidelined when there isn't a good way to "test" things to prove that they should work. Let's take a typical marketing team—one that conducts regular tests to try to improve daily operations or conversion. They may, for example, test two versions of an email to determine if image-heavy or content-heavy designs have the best conversion. However, these kinds of testing programs often don't work for the big investments—for a number of reasons.

Some tests are too small to be credible representations of the big picture. We've heard a number of leaders say that just because versioning an email by gender worked one time doesn't mean that broad personalization is worth the effort. They simply can't make the leap from a small case to the big picture. Big tests pose challenges, too. If you wanted to run a test to prove that integrating customer data and modeling the combined behaviors would result in better customer behavior, it may even be too hard to manually pull together the data elements, analysis, and creative support for detailed versioning—meaning your great idea will never get off the ground. If it takes several weeks just to connect data, and several more weeks to build a model, you may be denied the go-ahead from the get-go.

This isn't to say that vision and intuition don't matter. Gut is still and always will be an indicator that you're onto something. Leo certainly had a gut feeling that there was valuable, hidden meaning in their data. However, intuition shouldn't be the first thing leaders turn to, and is never as persuasive as proof. Successful business decisions get made through three means, and they should be in this order. First is by data—real facts and quantitative evidence, including company experience, industry examples, and case studies. Second is by experimentation—when data can't explain or predict, you need to try stuff out. Third is by leadership grit—after data and experimentation are exhausted, typically some uncertainty still remains. That's where judgment, courage, and determination come in.

There are a number of ways Leo overcame the "prove it" hurdle and got his organization to invest in new infrastructure he needed. Let's break these down into their Geek, Nerd, Suit parts and see how these solutions can work for all of us.

❶ ❺ WORK WITH WHAT YOU'VE GOT

Cobble together a homemade campaign or marketing test if you need to. Have your team manually analyze types of customer groups, and manually design multiple versions of marketing campaigns to send to those groups. It may not be sustainable or scalable, but don't worry—it doesn't need to be either. Even a lightweight, poorly executed, bootstrapped campaign can be enough to generate a proxy of value that business leaders will buy in to. If you are able to achieve any meaningful results with a poorly designed and executed marketing test like the one we described above, just imagine what you could do with the right resources.

❶ CONDUCT SHORT-TERM, LIGHTWEIGHT ANALYTICS

Even if action is impossible, analysis may not be. A fresh look at past results may yield proof that better customer data and personalized treatment matter. Start by looking at how different customer groups responded to marketing campaigns that you've already executed. If you can demonstrate that response rates are different by segment for different types of campaigns, you might have enough to estimate the potential value of personalization.

❶ ❺ FIND YOUR "BEST BEST" CUSTOMERS

None of your customers are giving you a 100 percent share of their wallet, which means there is opportunity to drive increased engagement even among your most loyal customers. It may be easier to get funds to support retaining or rewarding customers that are already proven fans of your offerings. Because your best customers are a subset of overall customers, it might be easier to leverage them in your appeal to get tests approved. After all, it's almost foolproof to suggest a plan for treating your best customers even better.

❻ ❶ ❺ SHARE THE WINS

If nobody knows about what has been done and what has worked, you can forget about building momentum. Start sharing previous wins from campaigns not tied to your current initiative to start getting people excited. Then, as you are able to bootstrap your way into new tests, make sure your wins are broadcast to the right audiences as soon as results are available. If leaders see that their decisions are yielding benefit in a short window, they are more likely to want to help you do more.

❶ ❺ LOOK FOR OTHER WAYS TO PROVE VALUE

If your own customer data coffers have come up empty, maybe external sources of data can provide support for investment. If you have a budget to work with, market research among current customers can also serve as a proxy of value. Even mocking up a type of personalized campaign and testing to see if anticipated response rates are different can be a powerful indicator of potential. If market research is not an option, consider third-party data sources that may be able to generally describe expected benefits from industry-wide terms such as "personalization efforts." Industry publications, case studies, white papers, or even user groups can be valuable sources of information that can take your justification from "gut" to "gospel." And if all else fails, well, you could always consider Leo's idea of creating a virtual world.

THE TAKEAWAY

We all know that you must justify your customer data investments because money doesn't grow on trees. The beauty, however, is that it should be getting easier to justify that investment because customer data is increasingly recognized as a valuable asset.

We can explain both the conundrum in the chapter and the solutions with a car engine analogy. When a new engine is designed, a manufacturer never knows for certain that it will accelerate a car of a certain weight at a certain speed at a certain RPM. Until the engine is built and tests are conducted, actual proof does not exist. But there is data that models the expected performance of that engine, and trust in that data as well. So they're willing to invest in a small proof of concept. Asking for proof that a new technology will drive the types of campaigns the marketing team wants to conduct is no different. Since the costs of building that CRM engine are quite high in terms of both time and money, you need to find data that is trustworthy enough to give confidence to your claims.

8

HELP, I'M DROWNING IN DATA

Your business is successful, but as technology explodes, you don't have enough data about your customers. Everyone around you is telling you it's all about the data. "What does the data tell you?" "Listen to the data." "Your customers are data points." Pretty soon, you hear the phrase "big data" and the pressure is on. You are behind the times. You are failing to innovate. "Without data, I don't think you know who your customers are," someone tells you.

So, you hire people and dedicate teams to collect data. In a short period of time, they collect dizzying amounts. In mere months, you have more data about your customers than you ever wanted, and you feel like you know them no better. Everyone around you seems to think you're doing the right thing—finally you have the data! But nobody knows what to do with it. When you look at even just a portion of it, it's like looking at the ocean from the beach—it extends so far that you can't see the end of it, data disappearing out of view on the horizon.

Companies often hire us to help them solve this exact problem, and to assess their current level of customer centricity—in other words, how much they are building their business and their strategies around the real needs of real customers. When we do these assessments, sometimes we find holes in the kinds of customer data they are capturing. They may have outdated information about one group, incomplete information about everyone, or no experience gathering or analyzing data about the needs and desires of people who engage with their brands.

But an increasing number of firms have the opposite problem. Rather than desperately searching for tiny droplets of meaningful customer information, they are completely adrift in a sea of raw and unrefined data, drowning in information. If you consider the number of customer interaction points and the types of information that can be collected at each point, it's not surprising that many companies are feeling overwhelmed. Just look at the sea of data detailed in the inventory on the next page.

The rise of "big data" such as the sampling shown on the next page is one major reason why more and more organizations are finding themselves struggling to manage and process torrents of new data. Every place where you have customer interactions, you have a new source of customer data that are captured explicitly (by asking the customer) and implicitly (through technology and analytics). The unfortunate irony is that too much data can create the same challenge as a lack of data: there's often no easy way to glean valuable insight from it.

SAMPLE CUSTOMER TOUCHPOINT DATA INVENTORY

RETAIL

- Transaction data
- Payment type
- Discount usage
- Name
- Email address
- Phone #
- Mailing Address
- Customer ID
- Loyalty #
- CC token
- Email opt-in

WEBSITE

- Account #
- Name
- Language
- Country
- Mailing address
- Email address
- Phone #
- Birthdate
- Age
- Customer ID
- Session ID
- Clickstream data
- Cookie
- Loyalty #
- Gender
- CC token
- Communication preferences
- Preferred store
- Social ID
- Ratings/reviews

CALL CENTER

- Customer information only captured on repair orders
- First/last name
- Mailing address
- Phone #
- Email address
- Master customer ID
- Engagement ID
- Call type
- Automated number ID
- Transaction data
- Unique product identifier (Repair)
- Communication preferences

DIRECT MARKETING

- Customer
- Promo lists
- Email address
- Links with embedded IDs
- Social affinities
- Alias lookup
- Promo response by customer
- Social network (associations)
- IP address (Organic search)
- Persistent cookie ID
- Sweepstakes
- Unique coupon ID
- NFC locations

LOYALTY

- Loyalty #
- Membership date
- Membership status
- Tier status
- Earning history
- Redemption history
- Program communication history

MOBILE

- Name
- Email
- Address
- Phone #
- App usage
- Logins
- NFC data
- Session details
- Customer ID
- Micromoments
- Search activity
- Purchase history

RESEARCH/3RD PARTY

- Email address
- Demographics
- Post-purchase survey results
- Satisfaction ratings
- Customer ID
- Geo-demographics
- Social activity

What problems do huge waves of data present? Wax your board and let's carve them up.

I HAVE NOWHERE TO HOLD THE WATER

Most of the organizations we work with have data all over the place. They collect customer information through a wide range of interactions (e.g., transactions, browsing the website, mobile app downloads, social activity, contact center calls), but that data is stored in different locations and in different systems, few (and often none) of which interconnect. Even if the company wanted to see what the sum total of its customer data looked like, it couldn't—not without embarking on a laborious and highly manual excursion.

WE'RE NOT MANAGING THE FLOOD

It's hard to think of a scenario where a company does *not* know that an onslaught of data is coming. In most cases, its arrival will have been preceded by years of painstaking arguments, business cases, and groveling on the part of the IT or analytics teams. But there's a big difference between knowing that a storm is coming and prepping for its arrival. Customer data sometimes comes in so fast and from so many directions that the company doesn't know how to start dealing with it. Faced with the options of fight, flight, or freeze, many organizations simply hold still and hope a solution will magically present itself. Unfortunately, immobility does not solve the problem. Instead, the flood waters simply continue to rise.

I DON'T KNOW HOW TO SWIM

Sometimes a flood of new customer data ends up unused and stagnant because the analytics team isn't trained or equipped to deal with big data when it arrives. The IT team may have built an incredible new system for processing large datasets—but meanwhile, the company's analysts are still using old-school spreadsheets and running queries through an antiquated database system. Modern tools are needed to support the task, and the analytics team needs to be trained in how to use them. Without the investment in tools and training, it's unreasonable to expect anything to come out of the data.

I HAVE 14 DIFFERENT BUCKETS OF WATER

In some cases, the sea of data can be so vast that it can be queried almost endlessly. Different teams within an organization might access different parts of the dataset, ask different questions—and ultimately get different answers. It's not unusual for multiple groups to study the same thing (e.g., the effectiveness of a new product launch), but draw completely different conclusions. Without an agreed-upon definition of the data, these conflicting "insights" can lead to political battles and poorly informed strategies.

Unfortunately, these sorts of problems are becoming more common as big data gets ever bigger and sources of data proliferate. Companies that lack the infrastructure and training that help make sense of major data squalls will find themselves forever wearing life vests. But organizations that make the investment now will be quickly rewarded by how much value they can find inside the data that previously overwhelmed them.

There are many specific techniques for managing big data, but they all boil down to the general principles of organization and simplification. Big data is only unmanageable when it is disorganized, fragmented, or unnecessarily detailed or complex. Big data is useful once it is distilled into its most important components, and when tons of individual data points are analyzed and synthesized into fewer aggregate data points. It's a bit like taking a giant pile of mail, throwing out the junk, sorting the letters into themes, and trying to create a story from what's left.

One retail client of ours had data coming from nearly everywhere (stores, website, mobile app, social media, research, and third-party data)—but it all went to different locations. To handle this disorganized deluge, they overhauled their customer data infrastructure across all brands and countries in order to collect all of their big data in one place. Then, they modeled the data so that it would reveal big-picture trends (e.g., whether customers were visiting more or less frequently than expected) rather than minutiae (e.g., customer 123 bought a purse on a specific date at a specific store). Now the retailer has a structured global customer database that can accurately answer any question about their customers. Although it's still early, the company has developed meaningful customer insight, improved their targeting and personalization, and increased retention.

You can start seeing these benefits, too, by doing the following:

Ⓖ Ⓝ Ⓢ GET YOUR $#!+ TOGETHER

The first step is to start putting your vast amounts of data in one place. The long view is to get every piece of data connected to every other piece of data. Yes, this will take time and a lot of work. Spend the time to architect a central analytical repository, and build a plan to populate and update it over time. As your centralized data store grows, so too will your ability to spot and act on the insights it reveals. Just remember: it's easier to swim in a pool of water than in a thousand small puddles.

❻ ⓝ CREATE A UNIFIED VIEW

After, and only after, you get all your data into one place, try building a consolidated view of your customers. Start by ensuring that everyone (and we mean EVERYONE in the company) is looking at the same view of the data. No more separate data tables, custom reports, or specific filters that vary by team. No more conflicting answers. *Customers do not change when different people look at them,* so you need to make sure that everyone sees the same thing.

❺ ASSIGN A CUSTOMER DATA MASTER

This may strike you as more of a Geek thing, but someone needs to be placed officially in charge of customer data to make sure it gets collected, and like it or not, that is the job of the Suit. Rules about what to collect and what to keep also need to be established and enforced. For example, what happens if you get a change of address notification from the US Postal Service, but the customer then logs into their account and changes their shipping address to something completely different? Which address do you trust more? A formal function led by the Suit, but including the Geek and Nerd, needs to make these types of data decisions. If the Suit abdicates, the Geek tends to take over and may optimize for their world—minimizing data storage costs and risk of data exposure rather than prioritizing potential business value.

❻ ⓝ ❺ CONDUCT A DATA INVENTORY

Once a data owner is assigned, have them start by conducting a data inventory like the one on page 83. How is your company interacting with customers, and what data are you capturing during each of those interactions? Which components are core, and which are ancillary? From the customer perspective, what do they most care that you remember about them? From the business perspective, which pieces of information can enable you to deliver a better customer experience? It may seem pretty fundamental to sit down and think rationally about what you're collecting, but almost nobody does this.

Ⓝ Ⓢ DISTILL

It may seem like heresy to mention this in a chapter about big data, but you really don't need to keep everything. As we previously mentioned, oceans of data contain droplets of insight that will change the way you view and treat your customers. They also contain tons of details with little or no real business value. For instance, dozens of strings of clickstream data might mean "Steven is shopping for a laptop." Distill the pure essence of the data from the total. You only have so much capacity to ingest, interpret, and act upon things, so focus on what matters.

Ⓖ Ⓝ DON'T UNDERESTIMATE THE VALUE OF TRAINING

Ship captains wouldn't be so handy if they didn't know how to read nautical maps, interpret the dots and lights blinking on their instruments, or steer a ship through a storm. Similarly, your analytics team needs to have the right skills for the task at hand. Old methods need to be replaced by new ones. Just as you can't expect a ship captain to navigate through a squall using only a flashlight and good intentions, you can't expect your team to uncover major insights within a sea of big data if they don't have the tools and the training to find them.

THE TAKEAWAY

Whether you're staring at a gigantic sea of data or a series of disconnected data puddles strewn across the organization, just start where you can. It may take a while to make complete sense of big data, but the goal is to keep making progress. Select a data owner and have them create a map of what the organization has and what it needs. Then, prioritize just a few pieces of that data that will help you make the customer experience better. The key is to have a master plan, but to break it down into manageable components.

9

WE DON'T NEED DATA BECAUSE OUR PRODUCTS ARE AMAZING

A few years ago, we worked with a big clothing retailer that wanted to create a more modern and youthful brand portfolio. They started by putting a "visionary" merchant in charge of the plan. Looking across the business's brands, the merchant saw ways to forge new partnerships with other well-known brands and reposition some of the company's own brands in new ways. These new brands would bring youth, energy, and a more upscale feel to the business. Accordingly, another recommendation was made to retire a long-standing company brand with an older, slightly stale image that we'll call Naples.

On the surface, this decision made sense. Why let a tired brand like Naples bring down the company's other edgier brands by association? In this case, the surface-level approach was easy to sell internally. The company's leaders understood the sales figures, so they knew what they would be losing. But the potential gains to the company's image seemed worth it. So, without even blinking, the company decided to kill Naples.

What company leaders *didn't* know was that Naples was disproportionately purchased by their best customers. These customers were shopping frequently (once per month or more) and using Naples to fill their closets. By removing a beloved brand, no matter how boring, the company risked alienating its most important customer base—and losing significant revenue in the process. Imagine, for example, Patagonia eliminating fleece pullovers—despite them remaining popular for decades—simply because they are not the sexiest item in their clothing line.

In analyzing the data, we projected an eight-figure annual loss— due not just to the loss of brand sales, but also to the anticipated loss of high-value customers and trip frequency. The company's leaders, now fully enlightened to the potential impact, considered this information…then retired Naples anyway. Their hope was that the new brands would, over time, fill this void and then some. A few years later, after continued declining sales and a large loss of customers, the retailer ultimately admitted its mistake and revived the brand.

So how could this happen? Why would the company decide to nix a critical brand even after fully understanding the impact it might have on their customers and their own bottom line? One reason is that these sorts of big-idea, low-data transformational strategies sometimes work in the short term. In our example, the announcement that a company is moving in a new direction, by eliminating a brand or adding a new one, can create a lot of buzz that, in turn, inspires a surge of new customers to check out the company's offerings. But that surge is often short-lived, especially if the company hasn't based its decision on an underlying understanding of its current customers' wants and needs.

Remember Crystal Pepsi? PepsiCo launched the see-through soda in 1992 as a "healthy" diet beverage, hoping to tap into the broad and long-lasting market shift toward healthier food and drink alternatives that was already underway. Although sales in the first year approached half a billion dollars, many of those sales were "curiosity purchases" that didn't result in repeat customers. Whether the company's customer data was inaccurate or ignored is hard to say, but the end result was that they misunderstood what customers really wanted—because a clear drink that tastes like Pepsi wasn't it.

When things are going well, company leaders don't always ask for or collect customer data. We worked with a client whose business had been steadily growing since its launch a decade earlier. Because the company was hitting its targets, nobody had ever asked *why* it was growing. But when that growth started to slow, they had no sense of what customer behavior was causing the decline. Were they attracting fewer new customers? Were active customers visiting less frequently? Were customers spending less at each visit? They had to scramble to figure it all out.

Having no data is not good—but an unwillingness to look at the data you have is just as dangerous as not collecting it in the first place. This "instinct before data" stance can occur at any level of an organization. Leaders might choose to make decisions without first looking at the customer data available to them. Conversely, team members might elect not to share data with leaders because they are fearful of delivering bad news—or because that data runs counter to their plans or instincts.

The collapse of the financial market in 2008 is, of course, a classic example of ignoring the screams of strong data. The mortgage bond market imploded because most were downplaying the risk signals—which were obvious if one looked at the data from the customer view. Many homeowners were behind on payments—more than should have been—and the situation would predictably grow worse once rate increases on adjustable rate mortgages kicked in. Not that this was a traditional use of customer data, but many were able to short housing bonds based upon it, making a fortune.

A more positive example is Southwest Airlines, a brand widely recognized for delivering great customer service. Whenever the company faces new competitive pressure or needs to respond to a changing market landscape, they turn first to their customer data, studying what it tells them about customer needs and then finding ways to address those specific needs even more successfully. We all know that airline companies struggle to make money. In fact, it often seems like a doomed business. But Southwest has managed to make a profit for over forty consecutive years. Their continued profitability is due at least in part to its ability (and willingness) to take customer data and customer service to the next level, time and time again.

If your company shies away from collecting data or tends to ignore what it has, there are things that the Geek, Nerd, and Suit can all do to help make customer data central to your future strategies.

❶ ❸ THINK PEOPLE, NOT PRODUCT
Product data is more prevalent than customer data. Most executives

can tell you what the top-selling products or services are in their business. When you ask for data to justify a recommendation (e.g., expanding a product line), don't let them respond with the product view (e.g., current sales of the existing product line). Product sales matter, but it's also important to know who is buying these products and why they are buying them. Get the full picture before you decide what to do. As a wise person once told us, "When a product doesn't sell, you can't ask it why."

❻ TRACK EVERY INTERACTION

No matter what your business partners tell you, don't deploy any type of customer interaction solution (e.g., website, call center, mobile app) that doesn't track customer data. That would be like inviting a bunch of people to a dinner party and not bothering to ask anyone's name (and later not being able to contact the folks you hit it off with). Yes, these systems are harder to set up. Yes, data storage costs money. But it's worth the investment. The best way to retain customers is to pay attention—and respond—to what they are telling you. But you can only do that if you are tracking that information.

❿ ❽ GO ON A WILD GOOSE CHASE

Instead of trying to force unsolicited data onto the leadership team, start by asking leaders if they have any pet projects, hunches, or early stage projects you can help them out with. Most often, these leaders will be grateful for an extra hand in getting these ideas off the ground, which will make them more receptive to data. Even if "gut" intuition is still leading the charge, when data is provided early in the process, it has a good chance of shaping the final outcome.

❿ ❽ TAKE IT THREE STEPS FURTHER

Don't just answer the customer question that you've been asked to investigate. Answer the next few questions that arise from that analysis, exploring and pushing the data to uncover something more than the surface-level (and often obvious) answer. For example, someone may ask what percentage of the company's customers have ever used a coupon. In response, you could also share the percentage who have purchased something on sale, purchased on clearance, or only ever purchased at full price. Further, you could anticipate the next couple of questions, too. How does this break down by customer segment? By most versus least profitable? Are there urban versus rural differences? Are there seasonal patterns? How far you probe depends on your understanding of the real business question *behind* the question.

❺ CHANGE YOUR AUDIENCE

Sometimes leaders will ignore the customer data you present because it contradicts their instincts or the strategy they've already decided to pursue. Don't give up if you believe the data is worth sharing or if it may fundamentally change a decision being made. Find somebody else who cares about (and will be affected by) the analysis. Eventually your message will resonate and the customer perspective will be heard.

THE TAKEAWAY

We're no longer in the era of self-dubbed "geniuses" deciding what to sell, how much to charge, and how to market it. And it's no longer acceptable *not* to know your customers; they simply won't tolerate that anymore. To bring customer data into your decision-making process:

- Use data to challenge a commonly held belief about customers.
- Never stop at the first answer—take it three steps further.
- Make sure data is from the customer view, not the product view.

- Keep sharing what you know until you find the right audience.

You may believe that a good product will trump anything marketing does. But good products rarely come from an absence of customer data and insight.

10

AVERAGES ARE EVIL

If you have one foot in a bucket of boiling water, and another
in a bucket of ice, on average you should be comfortable.
– Andy Laudato, CIO

We often quip that our company's slogan is "Averages are Evil." We use the phrase almost daily. Our company notebooks are emblazoned with it, and we even had custom Nike running shoes made for our employees with those words printed on the tongue.

After using it for years, you would think the expression would have grown old. But it continues to remain surprisingly relevant. Some of our clients have even asked for "Averages are Evil" notebooks to promote the concept themselves.

It's hard to pinpoint exactly when we started throwing around the phrase, but it might have been the day several years ago when we stood side-by-side with employees at a $10+ billion retailer listening to their new maverick CEO explain his vision for the company's future. He was charismatic, his vision was inspiring, and his presentation was full of data that seemed to strengthen his point of view. It was hard not to get caught up in the feeling of comfort that the data helped to provide. Looking around, we could see the crowd grow tentatively excited about the changes in store for the brand.

But when we heard the new CEO say that the company's average customer shops six times per year, red flags popped into the air above our heads. The more we thought about his claim, the more we worried about the erroneous message that particular data point might send.

Our client had given us access to their raw customer data, so we knew that the "average" being touted was extremely misleading. In fact, fewer than one in 10 of the company's customers shopped at their stores exactly six times per year. There was a huge group of customers who only shopped once a year, and a small group who shopped 20 or more times per year. Who do you think contributed the most revenue? You're right—the small group of frequent shoppers.

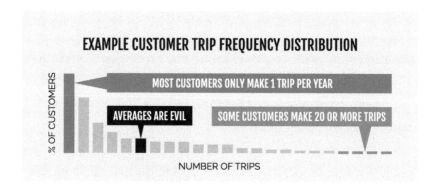

EXAMPLE CUSTOMER TRIP FREQUENCY DISTRIBUTION

% OF CUSTOMERS

MOST CUSTOMERS ONLY MAKE 1 TRIP PER YEAR

AVERAGES ARE EVIL

SOME CUSTOMERS MAKE 20 OR MORE TRIPS

NUMBER OF TRIPS

The danger of using averages to make business decisions is that it can steer you toward choices that seem wise but can actually hurt the company. The truth is: *customers segment well, but they don't average well.* If a 23-year-old millennial in Ohio and a 55-year-old executive in New York City are both your customers, how do they "average," exactly? A 39-year-old Burger King manager in Pennsylvania?

At our retailer, the average shopping trips per year statistic was far more deceiving than meaningful. Learning that their customers shop at their stores an "average" of every other month, the company's decision-makers might easily have assumed that product turnover should be done on a bi-monthly basis. They could have been so seduced by the "average" that they ignored the underlying data—all of which pointed in a very different strategic direction. As it turned out, the 5 percent of customers who were generating 25 percent of revenue visited almost monthly, creating a strong argument for more frequent—not less frequent—product updates. If the company had shifted to bi-monthly turnover, these prize customers might have become disenchanted by a product assortment that felt tired and stale to them.

Luckily, the company's executives soon recognized their "averages" problem. But we see the opposite happen all the time. Decision-makers accept averages as "truth"—and use them to make accidentally miserable business decisions. The truth is: using averages to better understand customers leads to flawed conclusions almost every time. Consider these examples we have encountered with clients:

- New product testing shows that, overall, your customers prefer a new product. But if you look at preferences at the customer segment level, the highest-value customers actually prefer a different, existing product. If those customers generate 50 percent of your revenue, then driving the new product might be the wrong choice.

- A report on the spending behavior of your customers shows that, overall, they spend an average of $200 per year. In fact, a small percentage are spending $1,000 per year (skewing the average), while the majority only spend around $125. In this case, the average masks both the extremely desirable spending habits of your best customers and the actual spend of the remaining customers, which falls well below the reported average.

- Your marketing team successfully identifies a pocket of customers who are spending $1,000 per year, and starts creating targeted communications for this group. However, some customers are spending $1,000 on a big-ticket item during a single store visit, while others are making many visits, spending more like $50 per trip. These two groups of customers may be equally valuable, but the messaging strategy would need to be different for each.

- A company that monitors only the final Net Promoter Score (NPS) to gauge the loyalty of its customers might feel content this score has remained steady over the past few years. However, a closer look might reveal that the company's "promoters" and "detractors" are both increasing at the same rate, suggesting that something is beginning to polarize the customer base.

- Two customers may have the same average loyalty program point balance over time. However, one of those customers has had only a single earning event and no redemptions, while the other customer has earned and redeemed every month. In this case, the "average" masks enormous differences in both the behavior and the value of these two customers.

As each of these examples illustrates, averages can obscure meaningful differences among customers. They also offer a false sense of security that "data" is backing up your decisions. At their worst, they can result in decision-making that is counterproductive to the growth of the business.

Why, then, does this problem persist in business today? Maybe the biggest reason is time: nobody has enough of it. It is far easier to absorb and accept the high-level averages being reported to you than it is to bushwhack through your raw data in search of more meaningful patterns. But given how erroneous and misleading averages can be, that extra effort is vital. A small push now for additional analysis can actually save time (and spare you a world of error) in the long run.

Also, many otherwise extremely competent executives simply don't realize that averages are evil. They have been presented with averages for so long, they have become used to these numbers, which seem reasonable and representative of their business. Few business leaders have been taught that behind every average, there is a *distribution* of data—a range of highs and lows that may look very different from what that average number suggests.

And not everyone has access to high-quality customer data. There may not be a capable or available resource to conduct the analysis, and the team may be used to accepting whatever they can get, so the numbers that come out of their automated reporting tools (typically averages) are accepted at face value.

Whatever the challenge, the ability to recognize and address the dangers of averages can create competitive advantage. Fortunately, there are a number of ways to avoid making "average mistakes," and the Geek, the Nerd, and the Suit each have specific roles to play.

❶ ALWAYS ADD A SEGMENTED CUSTOMER VIEW

Whenever someone asks for a specific data point (e.g., trips per year, most popular item), never give them just that data point. Instead, always enrich the answer by providing an extra view by customer segment (if available), or customer quintiles, so you can quickly see if there are any differences between your best and your not-so-great customers. Chances are, the answers won't be the same across the board. If they are, consider yourself lucky!

❶ ❺ ASK IF THERE ARE OTHER EXPLANATIONS

If you think about the examples in this chapter, many averages "make sense" and don't necessarily raise a red flag in a normal business context. However, it is risky to accept everything as it comes. The next time you receive a report on customer data, ask yourself if there is more than one explanation for what you're seeing. If the answer is yes, consider pushing for a deeper look at the data.

❻ ❶ INVEST IN ADVANCED ANALYTICS AND VISUALIZATION TOOLS

Averages are often used because they are easy to generate. They are a common fallback for organizations that lack strong reporting tools. By automating the basic reporting, resources can be freed up to do more data exploration. Further, these tools often have built-in capabilities that make data exploration as easy as adding filters to a standard report. Using visualizations to bring the underlying patterns in the data to life is also helpful. Most people find it difficult to see a pattern in a table of numbers, but will immediately spot it in a graph.

❻ ❶ INVEST IN ANALYTICS RESOURCES

Overreliance on out-of-the-box reporting tools can be a key contributor to overly simplistic data. As noted above, the best tools are capable of providing nuanced summaries—but they often require a capable user to set the right parameters and connect the tools to the right data sources. The best analysts or data scientists will be able to determine when to use a tool and when to conduct a manual exploration of the data.

❺ DON'T GO DOWN EVERY RABBIT HOLE

Teams have limited resources, and decisions need to be made about which "de-averaging" exercises should be conducted. When you're determining what to analyze and how much time to invest, it is important to consider two things: (1) how likely it is that the underlying data would tell a different story; and (2) how significant the impact would be if the resulting decision was wrong. You may not have the resources to do a deep dive on every data request, but you can start by focusing on the high-risk areas where it's most important to listen to your best customers.

THE TAKEAWAY

In the business world, averages are unavoidable and sometimes even helpful. But when it comes to understanding your customers, they tend to obscure meaningful differences in your data. All companies face limited time and resources, and if you find yourself relying too much on averages, we won't lie: it might take real work to change your current processes. But the reward will be more nuanced and enlightening insight into the wants and behaviors of your customers. You might be surprised what you find out about them—and how your strategies shift as a result.

Simply put, if you want to have average performance, by all means keep using average data. But if you want targeted strategies that have an eerie way of anticipating the needs of your best customers, it's time to leave those averages behind.

11

YOU ARE NOT YOUR CUSTOMER

Remember the maverick CEO who took the reins of a century-old brand with the dream and promise of reinventing the department store experience? Everyone was inspired and energized by his vision—the board, investors, employees. The CEO had spent long hours examining the old model. Then he'd systematically crafted a blueprint for the store of the future that would fix everything he thought was wrong.

One of that CEO's main gripes was the hassle and confusion created by the company's discounts, sales, coupons, and offers. Wouldn't it be so much better if everything was just one simple, reasonable price? No games. No stashing coupons in your purse or wallet. No waiting for a sale. And the company could stop sending so much direct mail as well—the millions of coupons, newspaper inserts, and sale notifications going out weekly. Some customers were getting old-school paper mail from this brand almost every day. *What a waste,* he thought.

He didn't seem worried about what customers would think of the idea because he believed customers would fall in love with the vision once they experienced it for themselves. Unfortunately, customers had no way to see or react to the vision before the company shut off the flow of coupons and sales. Customers started abandoning in droves, as was evidenced by the fact that in one year, the company hemorrhaged nearly a third of its revenue. And to this day, even after reinstating sales, coupons, and direct mail, not all of the company's once-reliable customers have come back.

In hindsight, it turns out that this particular CEO was not his company's customer. His idea of the perfect department store was very different from that of his patrons. They *loved* the sales and coupons. They *loved* getting mail from this venerable brand. They *loved* the thrill of hunting for a good deal, and the feeling of victory when they could stack a coupon on top of a great sale price.

More than that, many of his customers *needed* those discounts and sales. Much of America is on a budget, and they want to stretch their dollar as far as it will go…or at least feel like it. On average, the new everyday low prices were competitive with the old prices, even after sales and discounts were taken into account. But as we've discovered, averages are evil. Some customers—those who really needed it—were hunting for and getting disproportionately more of those discounts than others. They started shopping elsewhere not because they wanted to, but because they had to. While his vision may have been compelling as a new brand, it was too much of a stretch for these customers.

It's common, especially for entrepreneurial CEOs, to assume others will like what they like. If I think something is *so amazing*, won't everyone? Most, if not all, leaders make this error at some point in their careers.

Why didn't we sell through all of those neon orange skirts? I thought that would be the color of the season!

Why are so few of our top-tier loyalty members taking advantage of the free fishing lessons? I thought they'd love that! And why do they still feel like we aren't recognizing them for their loyalty?

I know that wine was a little out of our normal price range, but I thought people would jump all over a $120 bottle that you can't get anywhere else for under $180. Don't people recognize a bargain when they see one?

No, millionaire CEO, not when that "bargain" is 10 times what they would normally pay for a bottle of wine.

The flawed logic behind these sorts of offers seems obvious (and a bit ridiculous out of context). So why do they happen so often? One reason is the failure of corporate leaders to take into account generational, economic, or social differences to which they're desensitized. Just because a leader was once a 20-year-old doesn't mean he or she understands current 20-year-olds. Guess what? Today's 45-year-olds used *word processors* back when they were in college, and 65-year-olds plonked away on old-fashioned *typewriters*—and neither had internet access, because there was no internet! That's a pretty different universe than the one inhabited by millennials who text hundreds of times a day and take instant access to everything for granted.

But we can also make mistakes when others *are* a lot like us. Many product managers, software designers, and merchandise buyers have made their careers based on good intuition about what people will like. This works because we're actually not the rare snowflakes we sometimes like to think we are. We are products of our upbringing and socioeconomic class, shaped by life experiences similar to those of many others. If we like something, it may well be that lots of other people will, too. But, for every example of something we like personally turning into a successful product, there is the Ford Edsel, Crystal Pepsi, and Google Glass.

So how do we capitalize on the "I'm not a unique snowflake" principle, while still acknowledging "I am not my customer"?

One way is to let customer data speak for itself. Start by creating an integrated collection of behavioral and attitudinal data, including direct observation of customers' choices. With this foundational base of insight, the data will tell you what your customers care about, what aspects of your value proposition matter to whom, and what unmet needs you might address. Behavioral data doesn't lie. If you look at how customers spend their time and their money, you can tell what matters to them.

If our department store CEO had been open to consulting customer data directly, he would have learned not only that his customers participated actively in sales and discounts, but that his best customers did so disproportionately. He might still have believed he could create a better department store, but he would at least have been armed with the knowledge that he should proceed with caution, and take care not to alienate these customers.

Have you checked things out with your customers? This sounds obvious, but it's alarming how often businesses change products or experiences without first finding some way to ask the people they're changing them *for*. It's easy to do, and can be done in lots of different ways, from informal to highly structured. Focus groups, surveys, online customer panels, informal conversations, shop-alongs, ethnography studies, and live in-market tests are all examples of ways to get customer input before launching a new product, or making changes to your value proposition.

One retailer did a brilliant job of this. It's easy to forget that there was a time when large, flat-panel digital televisions were only sold by specialty, high-end home theater stores serving customers in the top 5 to 10 percent of household income. But executives at this big-box store hypothesized that there was a much larger customer base than previously believed for these televisions. They knew this by studying a segment of their customers comprising fervent audio-visual fanatics who frequently asked store employees about higher-end products and spent a considerable amount per year in their stores despite the fact that they were not affluent.

This retailer decided to conduct tests in a handful of stores. But to do so, they had to get manufacturers of high-end brands to agree to the tests. The manufacturers feared that a big-box store wouldn't be able to sell consumers on the advanced features of their TVs. They also feared a backlash from their traditional distributors, the high-end stores. In the end, a handful of carefully selected test stores received a limited quantity of plasma televisions...and sold through them almost immediately. As the test grew, it became increasingly clear: consumers were more than ready for these high-end products, and would pay the multi-thousand-dollar prices they sold for at the time.

We can now buy high-end digital TVs in many physical retail store chains, as well as online, and the prices are typically under $1,000 for larger, faster, higher-resolution TVs than those original plasmas. This is true, at least in part, because a handful of executives realized not only that their customers were not themselves, but that those customers had an unmet need they could fulfill. By creating a higher-volume market for these TVs, production costs plummeted, innovation increased, and the digital price-value curve took over.

Remember, leaders are not necessarily customers of the companies that they lead. When you have hypotheses based on your own needs and preferences, you need to validate them against customer data. You should also look for clues to unmet needs that you may not be recognizing because they're different from your own personal needs. And always, you should find a way to ask your customers—they'll often tell a company exactly what it needs to know.

Ⓖ Ⓝ Ⓢ BUILD A CUSTOMER DASHBOARD

One of the best ways to make sure everyone knows their customers is to keep a constant pulse on who they actually are. There are a number of continuous, largely automated means of capturing this customer information—brand tracking studies, online profile summaries, social listening centers, and appended third-party data are a few sources. Build a dashboard for executives that summarizes key customer stats, behaviors, and preferences, and make sure they view it on a regular basis.

ⓖ ⓝ ⓢ TAKE IT TO THE FRONT LINE—AT LEAST OCCASIONALLY

One step better than viewing data about customers is interacting with them directly. All leaders—but especially those in Geek-Nerd-Suit-related management roles—should spend at least one day a month in some way interacting directly with customers. Serve coffee. Run a cash register. Handle incoming call-center calls. It's one thing to paint a picture of a customer in your head, but it's another to be able to recall a specific set of interactions with named individuals. At one theme park company, corporate employees are required to volunteer directly in the parks during peak season. Not only does this help relieve the need to hire temporary staff, but it also fulfills a more important need to connect business leaders and executives directly to the customers they are trying to serve. Just be careful not to extrapolate a small number of interactions to your entire customer base.

ⓖ ⓝ ⓢ HIRE YOUR CUSTOMERS

If you really want your customers to be part of driving your business, why not find a way to hire them? One of our clients, a retail gaming store, does just that. Their in-store personnel *are* their customers—20-something hardcore gamers. And their customers know it. They love spending time in their stores, talking with like-minded gamers who share their passions. And it doesn't stop there. The most successful in-store managers can find their way into the corporate ranks, bringing the customer perspective even closer to company leadership.

⓫ GO ON A MYTH-BUSTING EXCURSION

One way to draw attention to your company's need for useful customer data is to find something that challenges a commonly held truth in your organization. Whenever we conduct even the most basic customer profiling exercise, we typically uncover something that surprises the team. A few of our favorites: "More than two-thirds of your customers have not made a purchase in the past year" and "Only 2 percent of your customers have ever made a second purchase." These are shocking numbers, but more common than you might think. Finding a way to shatter even a single customer myth can convince a company to take another look at customer data.

THE TAKEAWAY

It's common to think others will like what we like. For business leaders, this can lead to the misconception that they can satisfy customers by giving them what they'd personally want in a product or experience. If left unverified, this assumption will often cause trouble, and can sometimes lead to disastrous results. Preferences and needs are not universal, and economic, generational, and personality differences are likely to exist between leaders and their customers.

But don't set aside intuition and personal insight. Check it against the foundational base of analytics and insights that tells you what your customers care about, what aspects of your value proposition matter to whom, and what unmet needs you might address. Through their words and actions, customers are constantly telling you what they like and don't like, what they will and won't respond to, and what they will and won't pay for. Use both traditional and creative new ways to listen to your customers. Sometimes what they care about will surprise you.

12

THE CUSTOMER FOUNDATION WILL END YOUR DATA WOES

A central tenet of customer centricity is that relevant insight about customers should inform and drive many of your business decisions. But what does this really mean? There are any number of insights that can come from myriad sources—are they all equally valuable?

Remember the story in Chapter 4 about Karen? She's the CMO who told us, "I know so much about 50 million people, and I have no idea where to start."

Every company we've worked with has this problem to some extent, greater or lesser. Your customers are speaking to you, clearly and emphatically, every minute of every day—through their actions and words. All of this generates data, and all of this data has the potential to yield insights. Getting it all organized, structured, and aligned to your strategic and operational business needs is the challenge. Leaders tend to use the snippets at hand to address the questions *du jour.*

It's sort of like shining a flashlight on just the elbows or baby toes of your customers, rather than turning on the big floodlights to see them in full. Some customer insight is usually better than no insight. But taking a very narrow view of customers can create a distorted image of who they are and what they really want. And it can fail to reveal the really strategic opportunities to improve your business.

We worked with a beauty company that had this problem. The company's limited analysis revealed a core group of customers who visited often, bought more during each visit, and spent multiple times more than the next customer segment. The retailer assumed that these customers were extremely loyal brand advocates, and that their handbags and medicine cabinets were brimming with the company's products, maybe even exclusively.

Imagine their surprise when we connected the dots to a separately conducted research study, which revealed that these "super" customers were spending the same proportion of their beauty budgets on the company's products as their *worst* customers. In other words, their "loyal" customers were passionate about beauty in general, but not necessarily about their brand exclusively. Fortunately, the whip-smart and action-oriented team latched onto the new insight and immediately began tackling the problem head on. Inspired by the value of an expanded customer view, they found ways to strengthen their positioning. They implemented a plan that increased engagement and spend among their beauty-passionate customers, improving their brand loyalty as well.

So how do you illuminate the full picture of customer behavior and avoid accidentally distorting your data and drawing the wrong conclusions? You probably know what we're going to say here. It's by collecting the diverse data available to you, organizing it in a way that you can tie it together to see the customer in total, and using more varied methods to analyze what you come up with.

But this still isn't enough. Phrases like "data deluge" arose because this can be overwhelming. What's needed is a systematic and structured approach to putting this together and using it. Let us introduce you to the customer foundation.

THE CUSTOMER FOUNDATION

One of our clients had been growing steadily for years. They'd recently set more aggressive revenue targets, but they didn't know the best way to reach them. Was it by increasing brand awareness, improving purchase intent, growing the loyalty program, or maybe attempting to capture greater wallet share? There were executives in each camp. Our job was to quantify the value of pursuing each of these options, which we were able to do only after we completed a number of different tasks, including:

- Marketplace research to understand current levels of awareness, future purchase intent, and share of wallet
- Focus groups to identify barriers to increased engagement
- Behavioral analytics to understand current purchase path opportunities, and to estimate the value of increased loyalty engagement

What did we find? Averages are evil, naturally. There ended up being three important sub-groups of customers. First, the "Open

Relationshippers" were customers who were fans of the brand, but "dating" others as well. These customers were giving the company less than 30% of their substantial spend in the category, with key needs being met elsewhere. A short list of key product and experience changes would likely increase their spend significantly.

The second group was the "Lost in Translationers"—these customers had a very strong affinity for the key attributes of the brand, but weren't giving the brand credit for them. In other words, they weren't getting the message. The task with this group was to improve marketing in ways that would raise awareness of the brand.

The third group, "Past Lovers," had significant loyalty program activity and were previously more active, but of late were showing a significant drop-off in engagement. Focus groups revealed that the simple "points-off" nature of the loyalty program was not of great interest to this group. They were seeking more experiential benefits, and had begun to give more of their business to a competitor who had introduced such features to their loyalty program.

Collectively, following the strategies identified during the project, the achievable benefits with these three customer groups looked to be more than four times the likely benefits from any one strategy the company had been considering. But that's only the Nerd part of the story. Leveraging Geek and Suit skills in partnership with the Nerds, the company implemented treatment strategies against these three groups over the coming months that put them on track to reach their mid-term growth goals.

Having helped dozens of companies solve this same problem, we've developed a framework and approach called the customer foundation that works. It's not a software solution, a data warehouse, or "machine learning" (the shiny object of late). Instead, it's a set of concepts, business practices, and analytics that guide development of a knowledge and insight base over time. It starts small, and it never stops growing. We use it to help companies organize their customer data and build an ever-expanding collection of insights.

You build a customer foundation by first understanding its layers, then chartering a team (usually led by a data science or strategic business intelligence team) to begin organizing it. IT must be a partner. Research must be a partner. Marketing and CRM teams must be partners.

THE CUSTOMER FOUNDATION

DASHBOARDS		
ADVANCED CUSTOMER PROFILING		
RESEARCH		
CUSTOMER SEGMENTATION		
CUSTOMER ATTRIBUTE MODELING		
NEED STATE MODELING		
FOUNDATIONAL CUSTOMER PROFILING		
THIRD-PARTY DATA	CUSTOMER INTERACTION DATA	PARTNER DATA

It's easiest to understand the customer foundation from the bottom up, and it all starts with data—information about your customers, grounded in their interactions with your brand, augmented by any available third-party and partner data. This is the place where customer-level big data lives. It can be structured in a lot of different ways, including relational databases, data warehouses, Hadoop stores, and cloud repositories. No matter how or where the data is stored, the most important thing is that the data is cleansed and identified at a customer level, with significant history, so it provides a rich view of the customer's interactions with the brand.

Foundational customer profiling is about summarizing the basics of customer behaviors in aggregate. It captures macro patterns in purchase transactions, browsing behavior, loyalty program engagement, market research, and other data sources in order to set a baseline understanding of who your customers are. How many are there? How long have they been customers? What is the current retention rate? What percentage are shopping both online and offline? This is typically the easiest and most common place to start generating insight, and it has the added advantage of giving you indicators of where to dive deeper next. If you see through your profiling that 40 percent of customers have only ever made one purchase, for example, you may decide to conduct research to better understand what has prevented them from making a second one.

The next layer is need *state modeling,* which is about identifying customer needs so you can build a strategy to address them. Customer need states generally fall into one of four categories.

The first need state is *instant impulse*—real time interactions where customers are looking to learn or act immediately (e.g., when a customer is using their phone to look for a coupon while they're in the store).

The second need state is *purchase state*—a customer's current stage in the general decision-making process, ranging from ranging from research, to consideration, to validation, to purchase to post-purchase.

The third need state is *product replenishment*—for consumables, the need for regular replacement based on usage. This can be explicit (customer tells us they need to re-order), or predicted (estimated based on typical or individual replenishment cycles; e.g., the customer is likely almost out of shampoo).

And finally, the fourth need state is *need-to-know*—perceived or assumed needs based on business-driven messages, offers, or new products, such as a new product announcement in a brand we know they like.

In all four categories, the goal is to analyze customer data, identify which need state the customer is in (or is likely to be in), and use that knowledge to create a better customer experience. Each type of need state is important, and can be used both independently and in combination to aid with personalization.

The key is to ensure that we're basing it on what we believe are real needs, not hoped-for needs. Sending an email every day with a message based on a "next best action" algorithm is not necessarily needs-based.

The next layer up is *customer attribute modeling.* Customer attributes are the building blocks of a comprehensive body of descriptive and predictive analytics at the customer level. They are "mini-models" of customer behavior that describe or predict customer behaviors and propensities. They can be very simple, such as number of purchase transactions over the past 12 months, or time as a customer. And they can be more complex, such as a predictive customer lifetime value model, or a predictive churn risk score.

Because these models are computed at the customer level, they can be aggregated as needed—by segment, zip code, preferred store, etc. They can also be analyzed separately or in combination to find valuable patterns. Instead of diving into a giant database to see each individual's transaction history, customer attributes tell you about the behaviors most important to your business, such as number of visits, engagement in the loyalty program, marketing response by channel, preferred product categories shopped, and discount propensity. They represent a foundational way to *listen* to your customers by carefully observing, tracking, and quantifying their behavior. The more attributes you build, and the more comprehensive the underlying data supporting them, the richer your body of customer insight will become.

Once you start building customer attributes, they become extremely effective targeting tools. For example, marketers could use an offer response attribute to target customers who love discount coupons instead of blasting discounts to the entire customer base (increasing campaign response and saving valuable margin). That customer attribute could be combined with others, such as preferred product category and preferred communication channel, to further refine a campaign. It's no exaggeration to say that customer attributes lie at the heart of our approach to acting on customer insight.

The next layer is *customer segmentation,* which is about creating a view of groups of customers exhibiting similar behaviors—and we could write a whole book on this layer and all its nuances. Segmentation is simply the act of dividing a population into groups, and there are any number of ways to do it. Customers can be segmented on behaviors, attitudes, demographics, psychographics, and virtually any other variable as long as you have data at your disposal. Each type of segmentation has a unique role to play and a specific question to answer. However, what makes segmentation so powerful is when it helps identify your most valuable customers, identifies key differences across customer groups, and lets you build differentiated strategies to interact with customers across the board. We most commonly view this layer as a strategic behavioral segmentation that reflects the varying degrees of customer engagement with your brand. We also often refer to it as a lifecycle segmentation, as it typically captures the various stages customers might go through as they become ever more engaged with your brand. Basing segmentation on behaviors makes it actionable, since you can assign a segment to (and therefore target and monitor the movement of) every single customer.

Segmentation is typically too coarse-grained to drive marketing campaigns, personalization treatments, or product features. Rather, it is used at a more strategic level to monitor the success of your business from a customer perspective, and to set strategies for acquisition, development, retention, and reactivation across the segments.

And then there's *research*. While big data and behavioral analytics can tell you what customers are doing, only research can tell you why they're doing it. What's driving their behaviors, beliefs, and motivations both within and outside the brand? Of course, the options here are also boundless, and finding the right mix of quantitative and qualitative approaches is something every business will have to solve for. You might talk to customers directly through individual interviews, or discreetly observe them in their natural environments (by which we do not mean following them home to watch them open their mail). You might field online surveys or host focus groups. Research is often the missing piece that helps to humanize customer data and get team members excited about who they are trying to serve. In addition to a breadth of research techniques, a breadth of research topics should be explored. What is the current market landscape? What do my customers think of the competition? Why do some customers never come back for a second visit? Which new product would customers prefer? What share of wallet do I have with them? How do they feel when they interact with my brand? The more varied the methods and questions, the better your customer understanding.

Finally, *advanced customer profiling* brings it all together. At this layer, we now have need states, customer attributes, segments, and research to call upon. We overlay voice of customer data (such as Net Promotor Score), social activity, geo-demographics, and other supplemental data that can add depth and richness to our understanding of who customers are. The profiles at this level are very layered and nuanced, answering most of the "what" and "why" questions you have about your customers—and these answers can, in turn, inform business decision-making at many levels. These profiles can be brought to life in a variety of ways, from dashboards and visualization tools, to desktop tents and posters, to videos and other storytelling media.

USING THE CUSTOMER FOUNDATION
Generating insights in each layer of the customer foundation

over time helps build a complete picture of customer behaviors, attitudes, and motivations. And while each layer will generate its own "aha moments," some of the biggest come when you integrate insights *across* layers. Sometimes a seemingly simple business question can only be answered accurately by combining more than one type of analysis.

The customer foundation, fueled by great data, brought to life by skilled analysts and researchers, and put to use by marketing, customer experience, and product leaders, is one of the strongest elements of a customer-centric company.

Here are some ideas to get you started with your own customer foundation.

❻ ❶ ❺ COMMIT TO A CUSTOMER FOUNDATION

The customer foundation may represent a fundamental shift in how a company thinks about how to organize insight and analysis. However, a commitment to this framework will provide an easy objective for the team responsible for analysis. The goal is to add to the toolbox over time. The philosophy underpinning the customer foundation is to simply ask for any addition of data or insight, no matter how small. Over time, these small additions turn into some pretty dramatic revelations about your customer base.

❻ ❶ UNIFY THE LAYERS

One of the most fundamental components of a layered approach to creating customer insight is the ability to connect these layers. Deep understanding comes from studying how customers behave and what they think from a number of angles, so it's imperative that the customer data structure allows multiple sources of insight to

speak to one another. As one basic example, the ability to tie survey responses to known customer records can help you match the
"what is happening" to the "why it is happening" at the individual
customer level. It's the job of the Geek to ensure the data structures
enable that linkage.

Ⓝ BUILD A LAYERED TEAM

One challenge to building a customer foundation is that each layer
requires a different type of analysis. In our experience, most analysts are highly skilled in one particular area (e.g., quantitative research, predictive modeling, web analytics), but don't always have
the skills to cover them all. Make sure that your team includes individuals with a breadth of analytical expertise, so you're able to
generate each type of insight called for—and that those individuals
are collaborators, not just isolated experts.

Ⓖ Ⓝ Ⓢ CROSS-POLLENATE IDEAS

Even a layered approach to insight like the customer foundation
can create siloed teams and siloed data problems. For example, in
many organizations the research and analytics teams report to different leaders and may operate independently. If you have different
individuals working on different layers, create a forum to share results of recent projects, discuss the types of questions they are being
asked to address, and brainstorm opportunities for collaboration
between teams and types of analysis. Consider an "insight integra-
tion forum" with the sole purpose of ensuring the customer foundation works together to answer questions, rather than continuing
to leave insights to fend for themselves.

THE TAKEAWAY

While the notion of a toolbox of insight might seem overly simplistic, the beauty of the customer foundation framework outlined in this chapter *is* its simplicity. Lots of companies feel overwhelmed by trying to manage a complex spider web of unrelated analytics projects, which can get in the way of business leaders being able to use the insights being generated to drive change. With the customer foundation as their "north star," IT, analytics, and business leaders can all work toward the same basic principle: the more you know about customers—and the more you organize that knowledge into a usable structure—the better off you will be. No insight is too small. Start somewhere and keep going!

13

THE FUNNEL TO NOWHERE

We once participated in an "all-partner" strategy session for a client where nearly every speaker presented a purchase funnel—basically, a graphic depicting the alleged path a customer travels from becoming aware of a brand or product to ultimately making a purchase. We probably saw a dozen funnels over the course of the day. While there were minor differences among them—vertical versus horizontal pathways, slightly different lingo—they all shared a common trait. They were all presented in a linear fashion, implying a simple and straightforward narrative and customer decision-making process that goes something like: "I just discovered this brand of cola! I like the font and the can design! I will ask my friends if they have tried this cola! I will buy this cola!" The end.

The reality is that consumer decision-making is rarely that linear. Deciding to purchase something is a messy process that usually looks more like a plate of spaghetti than a straight line. The linear approach rests on the assumption that the story is chronological and the customer is merely a consumer. In reality, however, the narrative is often full of non-linear, non-chronological twists, and the customer is a unique character. As much as customers like to think they're rational—and companies like to think so even more—their decisions are influenced by so many factors that it's almost impossible not to get sidetracked along the way. Marketers need to be conscious of this meandering narrative as they're thinking about how to manage customer relationships. The length, complexity, and individual nature of these types of purchase paths make them difficult to accurately document. And, it's completely understandable that marketing leaders would want to simplify these processes in order to have a chance to play a part in managing them.

This is where purchase funnels are thought to be useful. After all, every product purchase can be traced back to a moment when that consumer first interacted with that brand, or how often they opened emails before purchasing, or whether it took them a long or short time to browse.

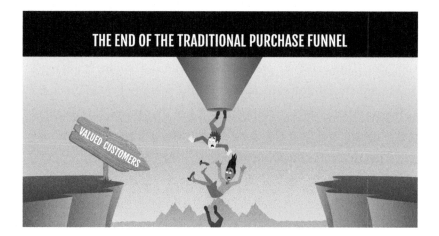

THE END OF THE TRADITIONAL PURCHASE FUNNEL

The primary drawback to funnel models isn't that they oversimplify a complex process. It's that they conclude the story at the beginning, the point of purchase, effectively dumping a stream of active customers into a nebulous pit that leads…nowhere.

When you think about it, the end of the purchase funnel is actually the *beginning* of the customer's longer-term engagement with a brand—their relationship. Creating a funnel that ends with a first purchase is like telling a story about a character who goes on a first date. You never bother to reveal if there was a second, a third, a happily ever after. And in business terms, it's the happily ever after we're really interested in tracking.

So why not expand the funnel into a never-ending loop of increasing engagement and interaction, where most of the effort is spent developing current customers and keeping them there? Awareness and acquisition are important to maintaining the health of a business, but what happens after that first point of conversion is even more critical. The goal, after customers are acquired, should be to keep active customers active—engaging them so they keep coming back, again and again.

Page 134 features our handy model for thinking about this never-ending loop, often dubbed customer lifecycle management. In it, customers are broadly grouped into non-customers, new customers, active customers, and lapsed customers. Within each phase, a company can develop and deploy personalized strategies that directly address the needs of that particular customer group. Non-customers can be targeted with brand marketing. New customers can be convinced to make a second purchase. Active customers can be thanked for their loyalty, and lapsed customers can be targeted with a reactivation campaign.

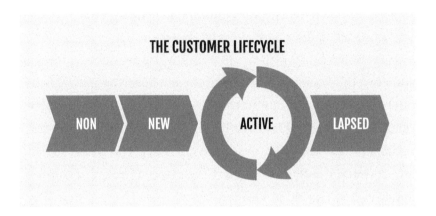

Notice that the visual emphasizes active customers? This is intentional. By merging acquisition, retention, and reactivation marketing into one framework, we are advocating that separate marketing functions should be integrated and aligned around the unified task of improving customer engagement across the board.

This seems logical enough, yet too often, companies—especially their marketers—focus only on one character and one part of the story: acquisition. They assume that retention and share-of-wallet development will magically just happen. Yet whenever we've studied website traffic, store traffic, and sources of year-over-year sales growth in mature brands, retention and development of existing customers—not new ones—are more critical. In a retail store, for instance, it is typical for more than 90 percent of traffic to be existing customers—people who have bought previously.

It's true that acquisition is critical to any healthy business. And for a brand in growth mode, acquisition is the primary focus. But for most mature brands, retention and development—the middle of the lifecycle—are the biggest potential source of incremental revenue and profit. This is where customer experience management can help the most. By ensuring that your active customers are enjoying their interactions with your brand, you can help keep the customer lifecycle healthy.

We have a client that treats this customer lifecycle management diagram like the holy grail. They monitor what's happening with their customers with the intensity of air traffic controllers tracking a sky full of planes. They welcome new customers to the brand with customized emails. Their best customers receive priority treatment and are given "surprise and delight" offers to keep them engaged. A "pre-lapse" campaign targets customers who aren't shopping at their usual frequency with a personalized offer to get them back into a store. They know where every single one of their customers is in the lifecycle, and they market to them accordingly. Not surprisingly, customer retention has improved year over year. Happily ever after.

THE TAKEAWAY

Traditional purchase funnels can be useful, but the most important aspect of the journey is tracking what comes after that first purchase. And for goodness' sake, don't treat subsequent purchases as if they were the customer's first. The customer lifecycle model shared in this chapter allows companies to view and track customers across their entire relationship with a brand over time. Rather than dumping customers into a dark abyss after purchase, this framework encourages marketers to think about how to keep those customers engaged for the long run—or how to reengage customers who appear to be slipping away. Customers might not bounce around nearly as much as they do if more companies paid careful attention to the customer lifecycle.

14

HELLO, WE'D LIKE TO REMIND YOU THAT WE SEND EMAILS

Every day, you probably open your inbox to a new round of promotional emails from your favorite brands. Lots of them. Regardless of whether you open these emails, never open these emails, have purchased items promoted in these emails, or have never purchased these promoted items, sure as sunshine, there's another email in your inbox the next day.

If you do read this deluge of emails, then you may have noticed the impressive ingenuity their creators employ in an attempt to make them feel fresh and compelling. Punchy subject lines, flashing emojis, or ALL CAPS messages try to nab your attention. Somehow they make day four of a 10-day sale seem almost interesting. And if a $10 off for every $100 you spend promotion doesn't hook you, they might dangle 10 percent off everything in front of your nose and see what happens.

This fire hose approach to digital marketing can sometimes get out of hand. We can think of several multi-billion-dollar companies that send an email to customers every day, promoting an absurd range of random products—from outdoor furnishings to bath gel to Easter Bunny decorations. While there are likely some pockets of customers who care about a few of those items, odds are high that no individual customer cares about every one of those products (and if they do, they may have a compulsive shopping disorder).

Aggressive over-communication isn't limited to emails. Online display ads can stalk you across websites for much longer than is effective, or polite. Have you ever accidentally clicked on a display ad, only to discover that every single ad you see for the next six weeks reminds you of your mistake? If the millisecond it took you to close the ad wasn't a strong enough signal, you'd expect that after a few days of completely ignoring the retargeted ads they'd take the hint. If a personal admirer exhibited the same behavior, you'd probably take out a restraining order.

Yes, it's true that this shotgun method of marketing will sometimes hit a target, but it sure wastes a lot of ammunition—and annoys or even alienates a lot of customers in the process. No matter how much customers love a brand or how many amazing promotions they offer, a single brand doesn't need to contact each customer daily.

Let's look at the language of some of these aggressively communicating brands. Our guess is you can probably identify with the following types of messages, all received within a month.

- Discover today's deal of the day!
- Huge savings on laundry detergent

- Read. This. Email.
- Sale on dining room furniture
- Big sale starts today!
- Only 3 more days of savings!
- Last day of the sale!
- Surprise! An extra day of sale!
- Furniture is on sale again!
- Kick off your weekend with savings!
- End your weekend with savings!
- All raisins on sale!
- Fresh new savings start here!
- Try our new home haircut system!
- Hop to it!
- Want to impress your friends?
- These offers won't last!

Customer attention is a limited asset, so don't squander it. How many friends do you communicate with daily? For most of us, it's in the single digits. And we have different frequencies of communication for different people in our lives. We might call those we are closest to almost daily, maintain moderate communication with casual acquaintances, and occasionally reach out to people we've lost touch with. Why, then, should it be any different when we're talking about relationships between companies and customers?

Every day, customers are giving you clues about how often they'd like to be communicated to, and about what. Are you paying attention to any of these customer signals?

- When customers last opened an email
- Whether customers have clicked on a display ad

- Whether customers own the item currently being promoted
- Whether customers have ever responded to a promotion
- Whether customers reported a service complaint yesterday, and might not be in a purchasing state of mind

Remember the customer attributes from Chapter 12? Each of these behavioral indicators can be modeled and saved as a filter for determining which customers to share your marketing message with. Layered with a customer lifecycle-based segmentation approach, you can really grow the IQ of your marketing campaigns. The goal is to modify your marketing calendars so customers get what they might need and nothing more—or less.

New Customers

New customers are still getting to know you, and are more likely to need extra educational information to orient them to your products and your brand. But they may not have made up their mind about you yet—so don't overwhelm them by storming their inbox in the first few weeks. A structured, thoughtful onboarding of cross-channel communications works best with this group.

Top Segments

Some customers love you so much that you need to make sure they know you love them back. Frequent communication with customers in these segments is fine, *assuming* you have something to say that is tailored to their specific behaviors and interests. It's okay to miss a day or two if there is nothing newsworthy to share.

Middle Segments

These customers are plentiful, and they like your brand. But they're probably not obsessed enough to warrant daily contact. Set a more reasonable cadence—like once or twice per week—and focus on messages most likely to have broad appeal or drive conversion.

Bottom Segments

These customers aren't really engaged so they're harder to motivate. But don't give up on them. Focus on topics that might get them interested again, like revealing something new or appealing to the category they previously bought in. Don't feel compelled to try everything, though, as too much marketing to this group can move them to "unsubscribe."

Lapsed Segments

You haven't seen these customers in a while, so you need to be especially thoughtful about how you get them reengaged. Re-permissioning campaigns and reactivation campaigns are your best bet. If they're unresponsive to emails, consider one last attempt to reactivate them through a more expensive, traditional channel like direct mail or with a promotion. If that doesn't work, be prepared to let them go.

Once you master segment-based communication at a high level, paying attention to the clues customers are leaving you can help you get even smarter about how often, and through which channels, you should communicate from there. For starters, simply watch how often they open and respond to your digital marketing campaigns. Further, pay attention to timing. Are there days of the week or times of day that work better for customers? Track these behaviors and filter accordingly.

Your customer database is full of information that can be used to infer preferences, including product purchase detail, visit frequency, browsing history, and more. Each of these signals can be used to ensure your content is as relevant as possible, and they can and should be used in combination. If a customer visits your website, carts a product, and then gives up on the search, an email reminding them about that item is probably timely, relevant, and welcome. If a customer indicates a preference for home furnishings and nothing else, perhaps you could channel your energy there. The point is to pay attention to what they're doing, and use it to inform your marketing communications strategy across all channels.

One helpful exercise is to map the customer's "interaction journey" so you can see how many times you are touching them via all channels over a given time period. The results can be surprising. Because channels are often managed in silos, little consideration is given to the big picture.

Take, for example, one of our recent client teams. We brought various marketing channel leaders together in order to gain visibility to the breadth and volume of their various customer interactions. Rolls of white paper lined the walls, and we started documenting an "average" month of communications for each channel. After a few hours of listening to everyone share what's going on—and many delayed memories of seemingly almost-forgotten automated campaigns—their leadership team stood back from the wall to see what we had uncovered. Their faces registered a pale sense of disbelief when they realized that all of their customers—no matter how engaged or unengaged—were receiving over 40 communications per month.

Paying attention to cross-channel behavior isn't hard. But letting go of the habit of sending indiscriminate daily emails (or texts, or display ads) often is. The "stop talking to them so much" conversation is among the most difficult to have with our clients. Convincing a marketer to reduce the frequency of their customer communication, even if only in one channel, can feel like asking an extremely thirsty person to sip instead of gulp. (In other words, good luck.) But after we run tests proving that certain reductions in frequency can actually increase response and sales (and improve customer sentiment, and reduce opt-outs), they are more likely to reinvest those marketing funds elsewhere.

One of our clients recently made this downshift, with great results. As a travel provider, the company understands that its customers have a fairly long purchase cycle. So instead of pelting potential travelers with vacation messages all the time, they just send messages during periods when trip planning or booking is most likely to occur, such as immediately after a long weekend or roughly a year after a customer's last planned vacation. By being top of mind at the right time, the company is far more likely to engage customers than if it had blasted them with daily messages about Hawaiian retreats and Himalayan adventures.

The Geek, the Nerd, and the Suit can all help to start "right-sizing" your company's customer communication calendar.

❶ ❽ TREAT CUSTOMERS LIKE FRIENDS AND FAMILY

You're pretty good at interacting with your friends and family, who are unique individuals just like your customers. Take a tip from yourself and start to think about your customer interactions the same way you think about personal ones. Figure out who needs regular communication and who can be contacted more casually. Start at the segment level, then add complexity over time by introducing variables based on individual customer preferences.

Ⓝ Ⓢ BUILD ANALYTIC MODELS TO SUPPORT PERSONALIZATION

One of the easiest ways to get started with personalization is to build the models of customer behavior that you're most likely to use as a basis of personalization. For example, you could model channel preference, discount propensity, preferred product category, preferred price point, or loyalty program engagement. All of these could be used to sub-segment customers into target groups with specific messaging needs.

Ⓖ Ⓝ Ⓢ BUILD A NEXT BEST MESSAGE HIERARCHY

What happens when you create customer attributes and still have too many things to communicate? You need to prioritize. We advocate a policy called "Next Best Message," which basically means making a list of all of the possible messages you could share with a customer, prioritizing them according to their importance and value, and moving down the list each time that customer interacts with you. This is more complex than it sounds (and it may already sound complex), so it's important to have a team you trust helping you to organize the content and make these decisions.

Ⓖ Ⓢ AUTOMATE WHERE YOU CAN

One way to avoid the tendency to over-communicate is to develop a calendar that automates the most important messages based both on business priorities and on customer needs. For example, a new and completely automated customer welcome series could focus on building brand knowledge and driving a second purchase. The content of these communications would need to be refreshed only periodically, as long as some slots for dynamic content are built in. An added benefit of this approach? Systems are far better at remembering the sorts of important dates and events that should trigger a new communication.

ⓖ ⓢ PERSONALIZE TO MAKE THE MOST OF WHAT YOU HAVE

Automated does not mean generic. Static content goes stale quick-ly and will inhibit your efforts to build natural relationships with your customers. Email templates, dynamic content, and retargeting based on customer behavior will be your best friends while you're forcing yourself to streamline your communications. Instead of blasting every message to every customer, personalization allows you to select just a few of the most important messages for each.

ⓖ ⓝ ⓢ LEARN, BABY, LEARN

You are maturing your capabilities. The marketplace is continuous-ly evolving. Some things you try will work brilliantly. Others will bomb. This process of refining how you talk with your customers never ends, you're never done, and it's never good enough. The best approach to this challenge is to develop a hunger for ongoing learn-ing and continuous improvement. Don't get so married to one ap-proach that you won't burn that mother down if needed.

THE TAKEAWAY

It's easy to see through a company's communication strategy when it's centered around selfish, business-led priorities, particularly when a daily stream of communications doesn't have much in the way of news to share. By thinking about customer communications in the same way you think about communicating with friends and family, you can shift your perspective and start varying how you talk to different groups of customers. They are constantly giving you clues about what they like, what they don't care about, and what communications they prefer. All you have to do is start paying attention. At the end of the day, fewer, more relevant communica-tions drive better customer engagement than blasting all of your customers with daily messages that very few of them want.

15

TEST AND LEARN SHOULDN'T HURT

It was a darkness-at-noon summer downpour. Thunder crashed irregularly as we arrived for a lunch meeting. After parking, shutting off the car, and hoping in vain for a break in the storm, we dashed across the street and into a dark little cafe. About two minutes later, Erica and Steve, marketing leaders for a client we'd been working with for several months, tumbled in, dripping wet just as we were. A friendly server brought some napkins over so we could mop ourselves, and we settled into a booth.

The subject of our lunch meeting was their nascent "test and learn" program. Erica, the Director of Customer Analytics (Nerd), was justifiably proud of their newly-functional customer foundation. Her team, in partnership with ours, was cranking out exciting new insights about their customers. Steve ran Marketing Communications. He and his team had been working closely with Erica's team to develop new tests based on these insights. The potential benefits looked to be sizable.

As we got into an enthusiastic discussion with Erica, congratulating ourselves and making excited and optimistic predictions, Steve got a bit distracted, and we caught him staring blankly out the window at the relentless downpour. When we asked him what was up, he said, "This weather." We nodded, admitting that long days of rain could make a guy feel down. But he shook his head. "It's not that," he said. "I know you guys are excited, but on my end, this situation is like this storm…I'm half-drowning most of the time, and occasionally I get struck by lightning."

Right then, we all realized we had underestimated the challenges of thinking and working in a whole new way. For now, it was a contained problem, but it could easily mushroom and potentially jeopardize the sizable benefits of our program and partnership. In this situation, all too often the response is to pat Steve on the back and say, "Hey, buddy, cheer up. You are great at what you do, and we have confidence in you. We have seen you weather far fiercer storms than this little squall. You can do it. Let's get moving!"

But that approach fails to acknowledge the real difficulty Steve, and others like him, are facing in a time of change. Steve was still executing all of the company's existing marketing campaigns, while at the same time introducing a plethora of new test campaigns aimed at sub-groups of customers, integrating messaging across channels. He simply wasn't set up to handle all of this change.

In a collaborative atmosphere, moments at lunch, chance encounters in lobbies, and quick calls between meetings are the places where the Geeks, Nerds, and Suits all need to remember that, ultimately, they're all weathering the same storm. In Steve's case, we needed to support him by jointly figuring out how to manage everything hitting him all at once. In this case, how could we add testing onto an already jammed workload?

Call us customer centricity fanatics, but we think every company should have a formal and ongoing process for identifying ways to improve the customer experience. It's one thing to make a strategic change to the business and then wait to see what happens as a result. But it's another thing—a *better* thing—to evaluate the potential impact of that change in advance, and in such a way that you can prove it will work *before* you proceed with a full-scale launch.

The simple word for this, of course, is testing. But when we mention the phrase "test and learn" to marketers today, we are often met with one of the following physical reactions: an involuntary wince, a raised eyebrow, or a blank stare. For the wincers, the word "test" triggers bad memories of late nights, tense meetings, unclear objectives, and confusing results. (Steve is a wincer.) The eyebrow-raisers are skeptical because they think tests can be easily manipulated toward specific outcomes or they've been burned with tests that haven't proven anything. And the blank-stare folks just have no idea what we're talking about.

When asked about testing directly, we've found that most leaders are supportive of testing in general—so they aren't ditching it or avoiding it because of an issue of perceived value. Some, in fact, may believe they are testing already, but the program may be ineffective because they are testing the wrong things. If a company sees value in testing, but isn't doing it—or if they're trying and failing—

it's usually for one of the following three reasons.

1. THE TESTING ENVIRONMENT IS LESS THAN IDEAL

Maybe the company's technology is antiquated and can't support the kind of testing that's called for. Overscheduled communications calendars leave little room for testing to happen at all. There are many reasons why just getting to the decision to test can be far more complicated than the testing itself. At one company, the marketing team had long been complaining about the difficulty of the testing process and the length of time it took to make a testing-related decision. They mapped out the entire testing process end-to-end and presented it to senior leaders. Imagine leadership's surprise when they learned that the marketing team wasn't exaggerating: the team's map showed it would take more than a year to go from idea creation to test result validation.

2. UNCLEAR RESULTS CAUSE THE PROGRAM TO LOSE SUPPORTERS

Poor test design, implementation errors, inaccurate data capture, inadequate sample size—there are so many reasons why tests sometimes yield ambiguous or erroneous results. In some cases, test results get invalidated before they ever see the light of day. In other cases, results may be trusted by the testing team, but not strong enough to convince business leaders that there's a "there" there. We've known executives who needed to see results of two additional tests before they would believe in an initial test's findings. Requiring tests to be conducted in *triplicate* before implementation added six months to the testing timeline. It also demotivated the testing team, making them feel untrusted and powerless to effect real change.

3. THE ORGANIZATION HAS NO FORMAL TESTING PROCESS

This is most often due to a lack of resources across marketing, creative, or analytics. It can also be exacerbated by inadequate technology or data that can't perform the desired test functions, or by an insufficient testing budget. Companies that make changes without a structured testing program are rarely able to generate predictable results. Even if they see improvements over time, without a testing program there is no way to tell if they are leaving money or customer engagement opportunities on the table.

In the case of Erica and Steve, the problem was a mix of these. In our rainy afternoon cafe discussion, we arrived at Steve's root issue: his team lacked the tools and capacity to sufficiently manage the growing number of customer subsets they needed to track in order to keep tests from interfering with one another. The proliferation of test and control groups was becoming unmanageable. This, in turn, created headaches for Erica's team, who were expected to analyze results and provide a ruling on whether the test was a success or not. Steve was also struggling with home-grown marketing communications systems that were unable to coordinate multi-channel communications. Managing all of this complexity manually was reaching a breaking point.

All of these challenges have the same solution, which is to find a way to formalize the testing process while at the same time keeping it simple. And nothing could be simpler than following the basic "test and learn" approach that we were all exposed to in elementary school science class. Remember the good old scientific method? We use something very similar in the business setting. It's called the customer scientific method. Let's walk through the steps.

STEP 1: ASK A QUESTION
The customer scientific method starts with a customer insight, usu-

ally concerning a behavior you want to replicate, or one you want to change. This can be at any point across the customer lifecycle. A well-designed question should be inspired by and arise from this insight, and it should be relevant and meaningful to the business. Also, the kinds of answers you'll yield must be able to drive meaningful change, even if that change is surprising.

STEP 2: DEVELOP A HYPOTHESIS

This step may induce eye rolling, viewed as self-evident or obvious. It's frequently taken for granted or skipped altogether. Failure to create a measurable hypothesis that articulates a feasible business solution will almost certainly lead to poor test design, misleading results, and wasted effort. Hypotheses should therefore be structured to include both an action and a result. Quite simply: "If [*we do this*] with (or to) [*whom*], then [*this*] will happen."

STEP 3: CHALLENGE THE HYPOTHESIS

This part should be the most fun. Who doesn't like to try to prove something wrong? But to do that, you'll need undisputable facts. That means designing a challenge process that will yield objective, unbiased data that either validates or invalidates your hypothesis. Beyond traditional A/B testing, don't forget to consider customer analytics, data studies, surveys, ethnography, and academic research. You may even have what you need within your existing customer foundation. It all counts!

STEP 4: DESIGN AND EXECUTE THE TEST

The test itself must mimic the assumptions and conditions in the hypothesis as faithfully as possible. You'll need to control for factors that might contaminate the results, and a documented measurement plan at the outset to squelch naysayers. How big do the test and control groups need to be to produce statistically valid findings? What data will you need to gather, and how will you gather it? How long should the test last? What defines success? These factors must be built into test design and overseen during the testing process. If anything unexpected happens, the test design team—including Geek, Nerd, and Suit roles—should immediately be consulted.

STEP 5: ANALYZE THE DATA AND DRAW A CONCLUSION

Be critical of your results. Enlist additional reviewers, especially those who may be skeptics, and respond to their challenges. The best conclusions are those that have been vetted by supporters and detractors alike. If your experiment validated your hypothesis, congratulations! Take a moment and reflect on your success. If your hypothesis was not validated, congratulations to you, too! A "failed" test is an important learning experience and provides valuable insight, even if the insight is to avoid doing something like that again. As Thomas Edison once said, "I have not failed 700 times…. I have succeeded in proving that those 700 ways will not work."

STEP 6: COMMUNICATE THE RESULTS

It is critical that your results get shared. After all, your findings can't influence future decisions if they aren't known. But don't just email around a spreadsheet filled with your data. Instead, compile your results into a simple, concise template that can be used from one test to the next. And don't forget to make it easy for others to see your "ahas." Give them your data, but don't make them sift through it in order to learn what you already know. Finally, make sure that you spend the time to host an after-action review after every test— whether successful or not.

Implementing the customer scientific method can be an experiment in itself. Try it with one hypothesis, summarize the results, then refine the process for the next experiment. The key is to start doing something sooner rather than later, as successful tests will likely begin to generate support for the process. That's the beauty of this method—the act of using it actually adds to its value over time.

On a cautionary note, some organizations that have formal testing programs only use them to conduct tests that are deemed to be "safe bets." In other words, they already know these tests will yield positive outcomes and a round of high fives. In our world of testing, however, we believe in failure. Not the "we risked everything on a single hand and lost the house" type of failure, but the type of failure that comes from pushing the boundaries with calculated risks. If you have no failed tests, you're not learning enough.

Much has been written on the subject of failure leading to success, so we won't repeat it here. But we believe it's critical to set up a testing environment where failure is both permitted and encouraged—motivating teams to try out their big ideas and making it possible for those ideas to pass through the approval process. Ultimately, the purpose of testing is to find insights that will improve your business results. The ability to fail safely and to learn from those failures will encourage teams to think creatively and take the calculated risks that may uncover the next big idea. So, fail away!

As we delved into these challenges with Erica and Steve, the storm raged on. We cancelled our remaining meetings for the day and decided to wait out the storm by talking through the challenges. In the end, we collectively realized that the organization was pushing them too far, too fast. By slowing down, going through each of the steps of the customer scientific method with care and deliberate-

ness, they could get things back under control. We also documented the top inhibitors to the process, and laid out a plan to address
them with better tools and training. It wouldn't be fixed in a week,
or even a month, but in a few months' time, we estimated we could
quadruple their testing capacity. By the end, Steve was laughing and
excited, and we all had a better idea of how to proceed.

Here are a few more tips that can help take a test-and-learn process
from loathed to loved.

❻ ❺ TEST THE SYSTEM

Before you get too far on your testing journey, make sure your technical infrastructure can do what you need it to do. Can you track
response at the individual customer level? Are your marketing systems integrated so you can create multi-channel tests? Do you have
dynamic content capabilities that can create multiple versions using
a single template? How much test execution is automated? If possible, conduct a soft launch of the test to ensure that everything is
working the way you need it to. If you can't do it, consider outsourc-
ing the testing before you pass on the idea entirely.

❶ ❺ GET YOUR TESTS UNDER CONTROL

Good tests require good controls. But what type of controls do you
need? Individual-test control groups work best when you want to
know whether a specific campaign or activity worked. Global control groups, on the other hand, are best for broad-scale measurement of the collective impact of all marketing and customer experience efforts over the course of the season, quarter, or year. In some
cases, both types of controls will be in place at the same time for
different tests. Make sure your analysts are designing these proper-
ly, or you risk invalidating your results.

N S SCALE THE TEST INVERSELY TO THE RISK

You may want to minimize the control population withheld from a test, particularly when you're testing the presence of something versus nothing. In these cases, the art lies in keeping the control population small while still allowing for significant and conclusive results. However, for certain tests involving greater risk, you might intentionally choose to make the test population smaller. By risk, we don't mean risk of failure; we mean potential monetary, brand, or employee cost. Generally, the riskier the idea, the smaller the test population. Note that as we learn, risk diminishes. Thus, if smaller scale tests yield positive results, you can go bigger in the next round.

N S START MEDIUM

Contrary to conventional wisdom, we suggest you ignore the low-hanging fruit and start with the so-called fruit at medium height. While easy pickings, low-hanging fruit may not bring enough benefit to the company to make a difference. Instead, select projects that are likely to reap large enough rewards that people will pay attention—and that will create real value if they succeed. Starting with something too big may set you up for failure from the start, so break those huge ideas into meaningful medium-sized chunks.

S MAKE FRIENDS WITH FAILURE

Unlike lots of business talking heads, we don't advocate *trying* to fail. But try enough things and some of them are bound to fail. Assign a "failure champion" whose job is to ensure that testing is achieving what it is supposed to and to track wins and losses. Give them a "failure fund" by allocating a portion of the overall testing budget to the ideas that are hard to estimate or model. This will allow some of the more provocative (and potentially game-changing) ideas to see the light of day. If none of them fail, you haven't tested enough ideas.

ⓖ ⓝ ⓢ CELEBRATE THE WINS AND THE LOSSES

Every result, whether positive or negative, is a chance to learn. Get the team excited about the prospect of seeing results. Period. Bring donuts to post-test review meetings, talk about what you learned, and celebrate that in most cases you'll never have to conduct that test again—either because it worked or because it didn't. And remember to look beneath the surface of failures for things to build on. A client recently tried an email experiment that ended with a negative ROI. Case closed. But then we noticed that the subject line they used generated almost double the normal open and click rate. The offer failed, but the enticement did not. Fodder for new experiments!

THE TAKEAWAY

Business decisions are based on some combination of three things: data and insight, test results, and leadership grit. The first is typically directional, but rarely tells us unequivocally whether a new product, experience, or marketing message will be successful. Too often, we jump straight to number three, saying, "I'm confident my team will make it work." But with the right skills and approach, testing is an invaluable method for reducing decision risks and refining ideas before rolling them out. Yet many organizations struggle with testing. Execution difficulties, lack of support, and a non-existent testing process are common challenges. Adding rigor to the design process in the form of the customer scientific method can start to build momentum. Be sure to test ideas that are grounded in insight and likely to generate achievable value. A focus on getting clean results is critical—ensuring test and control groups are adequate, and success measures are clearly defined and understood. Finally, creating an environment where testing is encouraged, scrappiness is celebrated, and failure is accepted will help the team build a testing muscle that will begin to deliver bottom-line results over time.

16

LET'S GET PERSONAL

Personalization is all the rage right now, and for good reason. What better way for a company to show it puts customers first than to tailor its products or services uniquely to them? But this rage is also becoming an expectation, and that expectation has created a personalization method in many companies that actually ends up alienating customers, making them feel misunderstood—accomplishing the exact opposite outcome than what was intended by personalizing.

Why is this? Because personalization is illusory. Brands and companies aren't people, so a brand can't really have a human relationship with a customer. And while some may criticize attempts at personalization as manipulative—perhaps even as dishonest artifice—we also have to admit that we, as customers, like it. The fun thing about humans is we're social animals; we want to suspend disbelief and anthropomorphize. When we get an email that says, "Hi, Brooke!

We noticed you haven't been back for a while," we know it's computer-generated, but we also like being called by name, and a part of us wants to feel seen and known.

But when the illusion isn't maintained, we flip from playing along to feeling irritated, or even offended. If that last email came as a postcard with the salutation, "Dear Brooke (or current resident)," the illusion is broken. It's junk mail. *They couldn't care less who I am.*

Quite often, in business and in life, putting in some effort often pays off, even if it's marginal. But with personalization, if you don't do it well, you're better off making the communications generic. For example, you're shopping on a clothing retailer's website. You put a few things in the shopping cart to hold them while you continue browsing. Then you make your final selection, purchasing one of the shirts you had plopped into the cart. So far, so good.

The next day, while searching a completely different site for a completely unrelated type of product, a retargeted ad pops up from the first retailer. *Oh,* you think, *they clearly know that I enjoy that brand. How nice!* But then you take a closer look. The shirt featured in the ad is the same one you purchased the day before. Uh, you don't need two of them. Then you notice that the shirt is on sale. Well, that stinks. You paid full price. After your initial disappointment, you decide to get crafty and see if you can get a price adjustment on the item. Invigorated and hopeful, you click on the link to the shirt you bought yesterday, only to find it's sold out and has been removed from the site.

There's a lot going wrong here. The retailer's attempt at personalized retargeting was obviously well intended. But the retargeting information wasn't tied to your recent purchase history. Instead of presenting an item that would pair well with the shirt you'd purchased, they tried enticing you with something you'd already bought. Worse than the loss of a potential incremental sale, though, was the impression this misstep left on a paying customer. *How hard can it be to figure out that I just bought that shirt and show me something else? If they can't get that easy thing right, what else are they getting wrong?*

Additionally, the personalized content was not tied to inventory levels. Everyone knows the old adage that to under-promise and over-deliver is a great way to satisfy customers. But promoting an item they can't have is the exact opposite—and it adds yet another ding to customer perceptions of the brand. *They don't even know what they have in stock?* In the end, the attempt at personalization not only made the customer feel like he overpaid, it led to his loss of respect for the company.

How do these kinds of experiences happen? By now you know our answer: failure to engage the Geek, Nerd, and Suit team members effectively. Each part of this experience was clearly developed and launched by separate teams. It was doomed from the start.

But here's the thing: a personalized element in every interaction with every customer isn't possible or even desirable. Most of the companies we work with have some form of marketing evolution roadmap that shows how personalization should build over time. The "nirvana" at the end of these roadmaps almost always involves having 1:1 communications with every customer, every time. But how realistic is that? Most companies today are dealing with millions of customers who are interacting with their brand in many geographies, through many channels, at any time of day, any day of the week. That's a lot of interactions to try to personalize, if you ask us.

So, how should we think about personalization? Remember the customer foundation we covered in Chapter 12? It is your friend in developing personalization strategies and execution. Research and segmentation can help you define overall strategies. Use insight about the broader attitudes, needs, and wants of your customer groups to determine when and where personalization can make an impact, and where it's not needed.

Once you know where you want to tell the customer you know them and what matters to them, implement simple but logical personalization informed by need state modeling and customer attributes. Need state models tell you what mission or goal the customer likely has in the moment. Customer attributes tell you their general propensities or preferences, based on past behavior. Together, these will guide you.

Let's go back to our web shopping example. For starters, the site should know that there are several key segments of customers, and each has a different personalization strategy. For instance, the core, most loyal customers should be welcomed back by name, with curated home page or landing page content, and relevant offers or reminders based on their propensities. If we know a customer is 4x more likely to purchase with a loyalty points bonus than with a cash discount, then offer the points. If they are highly likely to write ratings and reviews, remind them at the bottom of the page that they still haven't reviewed their last purchase and ask them to do so. Next, work on the re-targeting. Use Facebook or display ads to present products that are proven—via predictive models and prior experience—to be of likely interest. Get your offer and content systems tied to pricing and inventory so you don't make promises you can't keep. Is this hard? Yep. Your Geeks will tell you that. And if you can't reliably orchestrate all of that information, back away from that scenario and do something simpler.

We did a collaborative filtering analysis with a large client a few years back. We found that, at least in their case, the best seller in a category was the highest performing product to offer about 90% of the time. This tells you that, unless your personalization engine is *better than 90% accurate, you should just offer the best seller.* (Unless your customer has already bought it, of course.) Oh, and don't *only* recommend the top seller; find a few additional items that reflect that individual customer's preferences too.

And, as we discussed in the last chapter, a strong testing approach can help you find the right mix of personalization for each customer group and interaction. Regular experimentation should guide the evolution of your personalization approach.

So how can the Geek, Nerd, and Suit help ensure that ensure that customers feel like you really know them in the ways that matter?

🅖 🅢 REMEMBER WHAT I TELL YOU

If customers have taken the time to provide you with information about themselves, they expect you to use it. Everywhere and anytime it matters. Don't send an email addressed to "valued customer" after they've told you their name—it signals that they are actually anything but that. Be sure to connect your various data capture sources. If a customer provides her name to a sales associate who is using in-store systems, she'll expect it to show up when she logs into her online account.

⒢ ⒩ ⒮ DON'T MAKE ME TELL YOU

Often, customers are already telling you their preferences via their actions. Observe carefully, and learn from what they've done in the past. A customer's propensities are as important as their stated preferences. If I've been offered and refused a credit card eight times, let it go…at least for a while.

⒩ ⒮ START WITH WHAT YOU HAVE

There's always something you can do with the data you're already collecting. Don't paralyze yourself by waiting to have perfect data, or for some type of customer data that you think is better than what you have. If all you know is shoe size, great! It's always best to use what you already know while also looking for more compelling customer insight.

⒩ SIZE THE PRIZE BEFORE YOU INVEST

Personalization can be done in dozens of ways. Start by listing the points of customer interaction where personalization is desired, and then take an inventory of how many customers you will reach through each type of interaction (e.g., number of annual website visitors, social media impressions, and emails distributed). Next, estimate the likely impact of personalization at each touchpoint (industry benchmarks can help you with this). If you can't find obvious benchmarks, consider a rating scale (high/medium/low) that will let you set relative performance measures for each. At the end of the process, you should have a better sense of the value of personalization options so you can invest where it will matter.

⒢ ⒩ ⒮ DON'T BE CREEPY

If "averages are evil" is the rallying cry of data scientists, "don't be creepy" is the equivalent for marketing strategists. By which we mean: match your level of personalization with the status of your relationship. Save the more detailed stuff for customers who are more engaged. And be careful to avoid using certain types of customer insight—those things that people really don't want to think about us being able to analyze (e.g., changes in weight based on changes in size of clothing purchased) and those things customers don't remember or haven't told us (e.g., appended demographic data).

❻ ❿ ❺ MAKE IT REAL-TIME, SOMETIMES

Personalization can be costly, especially if real-time data, significant creative versioning, and quick decision-making are required. The reality is that consumers expect you to know them in specific contexts (e.g., I just put that item in my cart), but not in others (e.g., a store employee doesn't need to know that I just did a search on my mobile app). Be smart about where you spend the energy it takes to get real-time right.

THE TAKEAWAY

Personalization is a customer expectation that is here to stay. The trick is to know when to get personal. Remember:

- Keep personalization on your roadmap, but know that 1:1 communication all the time is not possible or necessary.
- Each layer of the customer foundation provides insight that can be used to drive personalization—from strategy to experience design to execution.
- Since personalization takes time and money, identify where personalization matters to customers the most and start there.
- Personalization is a spectrum. There are times when mass communication is not only okay, but also preferable.

17

MARKETING IS JUST THE INVITATION TO THE PARTY

At one of our Fortune 100 retail clients, we got into the habit of holding weekly meetings with the president, chief marketing officer, and chief information officer. The discussions were lively and thought-provoking, and almost always centered on the intersection of marketing, analytics, and technology. One week, we clearly walked in on the aftermath of an "impassioned" discussion between these three guys. The CMO had suggested some tweaks to a technology platform that the CIO clearly felt was his turf. The CIO, in so many words, told him to stop worrying about IT and just focus on driving traffic to the store. In reply, the CMO offered a wry smile and a few choice words. "Marketing is just the *invitation* to the party," the CMO said. "But what happens at the party itself is something we all own."

It was a casual comment and wasn't belabored, but it stuck with us. Pretty much everyone would agree that marketing's primary function is to create brand awareness and demand in order to drive customers toward a company's products and services. Sometimes, that means finding creative ways to get would-be customers excited about the brand. In other cases, it's about offering education, making sure everyone has the info they need to make good decisions, or tapping into a latent need—something the customer wasn't aware of, but once aware, suddenly can't live without. Ultimately, marketing reflects a company's promise to customers and sets their expectations about the customer experience that's about to unfold. In other words, marketing needs to get the guests to the party, but they can't guarantee those guests will have a good time once they get there.

However, there is one great way you can ensure that guests will have a rotten time. You advertise free drinks, and then charge them a mint for cups. You promise shrimp and caviar, and serve them crackers and spreadable cheese. In other words, you lure customers under false pretenses. While shady marketing tactics or misleading content can sometimes have a short-term payoff, they are pretty disastrous in the long term. See if any of these "fabulous" offerings sound familiar:

- A hot new app offers you a free download, but almost anything within the app costs money, including the privilege of not being bombarded by constant advertising.
- A home contractor gives you an estimate that meets your deadline and is reasonably priced, but the final delivery and invoice still manage to exceed even your worst expectations.
- A cellular provider claims the best reliability in the nation, but after switching you experience just as many dropped calls as

you did before.

- In the subject line of an email, one of your favorite companies declares that you've just won a free trip. But then you read
through a novel's worth of disclaimers, only to learn that a purchase is required in order to collect your "free" vacation.

Let's face it: customers might show up for one bad party, but they
won't come back to the Emerald City. That's why creating the right
kind of invitation—one that intrigues and illuminates in just the
right (and honest) ways—is critical to getting potentially loyal,
long-term customers through the front door. And this is where the
handoff from marketing to customer experience happens.

We've talked in general about customer experience throughout this
book. But it's important to emphasize here just how many interactions and touchpoints are bundled inside that phrase—everything
from a friendly employee at checkout and a personalized thank you
for making a purchase to a slick new mobile app that makes shopping
a breeze. While each of these events counts as a single impression,
the true customer experience is a composite of every interaction
one has with a company. And everyone in the organization—from
marketing to IT—has a hand in creating that experience.

If you look at the visual on page 170, you can see how marketing is
just one component in the party mix. Product, delivery, and customer support also have important roles to play. Your brand should
serve as a filter that shapes how you present each of the four components of your experience to customers. Finally, customer data
should be fueling the execution of each. All of these components
need to work together to create an ideal end-to-end customer
experience.

THE CUSTOMER EXPERIENCE FILTER

CUSTOMER EXPERIENCE

BRAND

MARKETING	360° VIEW OF THE CUSTOMER	PRODUCTS & SERVICES
DELIVERY		SUPPORT

BRAND

CUSTOMER EXPERIENCE

Let's start with *marketing*—the invitation to the party. The way that marketing approaches customers—from choice of words and visual elements to the tone and vibe of each communication—lets customers know exactly what to expect at the party. If you get a frilly pink invitation in the mail, slapped everywhere with unicorn stickers and written out in glitter ink, you probably don't think: *Must be a football party.* It is marketing's responsibility to make sure that what is promised to customers is both compelling and accurate.

In the upper right, you have the heart of the party: *products and services.* Although we know that every component in the customer experience matters, this is what customers really came for—it better live up to their expectations. Everything you promise to customers through marketing must be embodied in what you give them, or their experience will be less than stellar. There's no good party with bad products.

In the bottom left is *delivery*. This category includes all the elements of customer experience that arise from the delivery of a product or service to a customer, such as store ambiance, quality of packaging, or speed of delivery. Sometimes these elements are hard to separate from the product itself. Is a flight attendant's friendly greeting part of the service offered by an airline? How about the in-flight snack or amount of legroom? Regardless of where you draw the line, these experiential details play a critical part in determining whether the party lives up to the invitation.

The final quadrant, *support,* refers to all the ways that customers seek and receive assistance, from launching a live "help" chat on a company's website to phone calls and FAQs. No product or service is perfect. How a company helps people who have questions or issues, and how it recovers from its mistakes, are critically important to establishing and maintaining great customer experience.

Of course, doing any of these things is far harder if you're missing the two remaining rectangles encircling the visual: *customer experience* and *brand*. Without insight, that critical frontline of marketing is flying blind. And without brand, the customer experience would be running without a north star, resulting in a disjointed and lackluster experience.

The recurring theme here with customer centricity—and also with marketing—is that everything comes back to knowing your customer: who they are, what they value in your brand, what needs your products or services are meeting for them, how they want to interact with you, and what they expect when something goes wrong. It's not enough to send a great invitation. The *entire experience* has to be great.

Some companies really get this right. Patagonia, from their superior products, to their lifetime warranty, to their integrity to environmental values, shows us how a company can continue to synthesize every element of their business to create customer centricity.

Disney theme parks promise they'll deliver a magical family experience, and they nearly always do. Their success is due to a combination of complete alignment to a specific goal (making it the "Happiest Place on Earth") and a willingness to look at the end-to-end experience. From the minute you land until the minute you leave, every aspect of the visit has been cultivated.

Starbucks was founded on a differentiated customer experience. Initially, they were focused on creating a comfortable and relaxing environment where consumers could spend time in "the third place." But they still continue to find ways to innovate in their space and maintain that edge—like by adding efficiency-maximizing and stress-reducing features of that experience, including drive-thru windows and the ability to order and pay in-app. Marketing has played a key role in this evolution, inviting customers at every turn to experience new offerings and features while reinforcing that the party will still be the one they expect.

If you're ready to move beyond great marketing into an orchestrated customer experience that includes marketing, product, support, delivery, customer insight, and brand, here are a few tips to get you started.

❶ ❺ MAP THE GAPS AND THE BRIDGES

Journey mapping can be an effective tool in understanding what is working—and what isn't—for customers. It's critical to ensure your journey maps cover every aspect of the customer experience, not just the marketing components and other obvious touchpoints along the purchase path like speed of checkout or ease of finding a product. Look at the places where customers get stuck, frustrated, or lost; the frequency and personalization of communications; the quality of and satisfaction with your products; and your ability to resolve issues when they arise. Figure out which touchpoints are working the best, and why that is. You'll learn a lot from both approaches.

ⓞ ⓢ DREAM PARTY

What does your brand's ideal customer experience look like? Tell the story you'd love to convey via your marketing messages without being dishonest about your product. A creative marketer always knows that he or she can't make lemonade with kumquats, no matter how they're spun. What promise could you deliver without the slightest worry that the invitation will be better than the party? Then systematically go through your existing experience, and identify the places where the current party falls short. Challenge yourself and your organization to attack that list, changing what needs to be changed to create seamlessness between what you promise and what you deliver.

ⓖ MAKE MARKETING TECHNOLOGY EARN ITS PAYCHECK

By now, you probably know that having great marketing technology makes data collection, analysis, and automation significantly easier. Now it's time to ensure that same technology is working hard to improve your customers' lives as well. Make it easy for customers to give you the data that matters, and then *remember what they tell you*. Offer ways for them to find the information or help they need quickly. The best marketing technology should help customers at least as much as it helps you.

ⓃⓈ THROW A BUNCH OF SMALL PARTIES

Chances are your products and services are purchased by a fairly diverse group of people. If you try to design a party that all of those people will love, you're going to end up with either a totally boring and generic shindig or a party that's trying to do so many things at once that everyone is confused (think: polka music, '80s pop, and heavy metal all being performed simultaneously). Instead, it's a better bet to design smaller parties that meet the specific needs of specific customer groups. This could be as simple as differentiated marketing and as complex as designing a dynamic pricing model that considers individual price sensitivity.

ⓃⓈ FIND THE RIGHT PEOPLE

Each of your small parties will need the right guests (e.g., don't invite metal heads to a polka festival). The size of each party may differ greatly, and so might the execution. But at its core, this is a matchmaking job. Learn what matters to your customers—which products they like, what offers motivate them—and then mingle. Start talking to them about this stuff specifically. These sorts of focused efforts will begin to grab attention—and get even more well-fitting customers to come to your party.

THE TAKEAWAY

It's the job of marketing to generate as much excitement about a brand as possible. But it's everyone's job to ensure coherence between the promises they create and the experiences the brand delivers. Getting "the right people to the right party" isn't enough. A customer-centric company applies what it's learning about customers to marketing, customer experience delivery, and its products—and keeps them aligned. By doing this, you can avoid situations where what you deliver to customers doesn't live up to their expectations.

18

LOYALTY IS NOT A PROGRAM

You probably have a stack of old-school loyalty program cards in a drawer somewhere, or perhaps a relic or two swinging on your keychain. Maybe you just have an inbox that fills up regularly with special loyalty rewards offers. You are not alone. Each year, more and more customers join loyalty programs, and millions of dollars in sales are triggered by these memberships. But having a loyalty program does not always mean having loyal customers.

We worked with a company that raved about its loyalty program. "We practically invented the modern loyalty program," they boasted. Launched back in the 1990s, tens of millions of customers belonged to it. The company had set up their systems so that loyalty program members would be identified as such whenever they made a purchase. As a result, they knew for sure that most of their sales were tied to these members. Did you catch that? "Nearly all of our revenue comes from our program members," they told us. Now, what could be more loyal than that?

When we looked at their program, we noticed that, while some program members shopped with them multiple times a month, others visited just once a year. Moreover, the variations in their spending patterns were pretty significant, ranging from single-digit dollars to $1,000 per visit.

They had also run several focus groups designed to capture members' thoughts about the loyalty program and the brand. Expecting their customers to mirror their own enthusiasm, imagine their surprise when they learned that about half of the members recruited to participate *weren't even aware they were in the loyalty program*. Worse still, almost nobody in the room could describe its benefits. Imagine a marriage counselor asking your spouse what he loves about your marriage, and he says, "We got married?" When the company followed up on these revelations with quantitative research, they confirmed that program awareness was moderate, knowledge of benefits was poor, and rewards earning and redemption were abysmal. Does that sound like a passionate marriage to you?

Before this is taken as an unfair bashing of loyalty programs (which, we assure you, it is not), we want to clarify that loyalty programs play an important role in many organizations' customer engagement strategies—and they can be a phenomenally effective way to capture customer information and reward your best customers. When offered a big discount just for joining a program, many customers have no problem telling you all about themselves. And, some programs do a great job of making members feel special and acknowledged for truly being loyal.

However, traditional loyalty programs are facing new challenges these days—and many are struggling to stay relevant. Customers today typically belong to dozens of loyalty programs. It's hard enough for them to keep different program benefits and details straight, and even harder to be loyal to or advocates of that many brands.

Consumers have also caught on to the fact that some loyalty programs are merely thinly veiled ploys to figure out who you are so they can stalk you with inconvenient marketing and promotions. In response, they're getting more demanding about what companies need to offer in return for their personal information.

Finally, many standard loyalty programs are starting to feel just that—standard. Too often, that standard is starting to resemble a trap rather than a key to the VIP room. The ubiquity of traditional points-based programs means they aren't differentiating brands like they used to. The earning structures and reward options can feel so similar that it's getting harder for brands to stick out.

So what is a company to do? When we work with organizations that have loyalty programs, our first piece of advice is to start thinking about "loyalty" in two different categories, small and big. Small loyalty is the loyalty program itself, which will continue to play an important role in the consumer decision-making process. Big loyalty, on the other hand, is the type of trusted relationship that you earn after continuously and faithfully delivering on your brand promise. Small loyalty's first priority should always be generating big loyalty. If a program goal of generating data comes first, for example, small loyalty runs the risk of eroding big loyalty.

Let's start by tackling small loyalty. Loyalty programs have had a long run of helping companies attract and retain customers. Almost two decades ago, Bain & Company found that a 5% increase in customer retention can boost profits anywhere from 25% to 95%, and it's still true today. With a limited marketing budget, it just makes sense for companies to spend resources on ensuring the customers they already have are happy and loyal.

When designed well, loyalty programs can serve some important functions. They often do a great job of giving customers a reason to self-identify. Tracking customers' purchases so they can earn rewards is often enough to ensure they raise their hand every time they visit. These programs can also generate customer aspiration, particularly if tiered benefits structures reward them more heavily for advanced levels of spending. Just think about how quickly airline program miles begin to accrue when you start earning the mileage bonuses at the highest tiers. They can also improve the quality of the customer experience, particularly if members are privy to special apps, expedited lines, programs, or services that make their experience feel exclusive.

The danger comes when companies forget that customer engagement—big loyalty—comes from so much more than just loyalty program membership. As you can see from the chart on page 181, making a purchase is the second-lowest form of commitment a customer makes to a brand, and providing an email or joining a loyalty program ranks only modestly higher. True loyalty often comes much later, after customers have interacted with a brand, tried its products, and experienced its customer service.

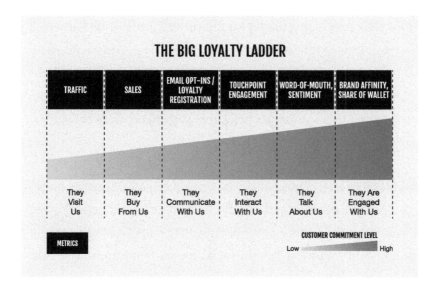

Customer relationships start with some form of exploration of the brand—often in the form of "traffic." Customers visit your website or walk into your store to check you out. While there may be some indicators at this stage of the potential for a customer relationship to form—such as how often they swing by or how long they browse—there is no commitment yet. Customers are still making up their minds about you and what you're offering.

The next level of loyalty is reached when a customer makes a purchase. Shelling over some dough to buy something from you is low on the ladder because all it really indicates is that what you sold met a specific need at a single point in time. This reinforces the point that relationship development can't stop at the point of conversion. Rather, it needs to *start* there. Otherwise, true loyalty will never be achieved.

Commitment from a customer begins when they give you some data. Maybe they offered an email address you can use to communicate with them, or joined a loyalty program that they know will allow you to keep tabs on their behavior over time. Although emails can be shared and loyalty programs can be joined pre-purchase, the fact that customers have started to share personal information with you qualifies this as a higher level of engagement. They've told you they want you to know who they are.

This is where engagement really starts to accelerate. Touchpoint interactions are those instances where customers start reaching out directly to you. They are now opening your emails, using your mobile app, and following you on social media. They are making the first move.

If they like you enough, they move to the next phase—brand advocacy. They are broadly happy with how things are going, and their overall satisfaction is high. They say good things about you when asked, and eventually they start saying good things about you unprompted. Pretty soon they'll be telling their mothers about you!

At the end of the spectrum is a truly engaged customer—one who prefers your brand over others and allocates a disproportionate share of their category spend to your brand. This is the holy grail of customer engagement—true love—and it doesn't come without hard work and intentional management of customer interactions along the way.

But wait. Isn't the goal of business to close sales? Getting cash from a customer is the whole point, right? Why should you care about those higher levels of engagement? Remember what we said earlier about retention rates and cost of acquisition? It's typically much easier to get an additional sale from someone who has already bought

from you than someone who hasn't. Businesses that effectively retain customers are far more profitable than those that don't, and
engagement creates real and intangible switching costs. Loyalty isn't
just a moral virtue; it's a commercial virtue as well.

Building a loyal customer base requires creating interactions that
are experiential, not just transactional. And since experiences are
consumed at the individual level, knowledge of your individual
customers is critical here. You should know their implicit and
explicit preferences and manage their experience accordingly.
In other words, watch what they do and listen to what they tell
you. Then, make sure you use that knowledge to customize their
experience.

Take the Starwood Preferred Guest experience as an example. Once
you're Platinum, every single interaction with Starwood is gilded in
platinum, from hotel check-ins to call center interactions to email
communications. If you always request a certain type of bed, they
default your bookings to receive that type of bed. If you always ask
for the 500 Starpoints at check-in instead of a welcome treat, they
remember that and just quickly confirm that your preference hasn't
changed. Their service personnel are very well trained to make their
preferred guests feel special. There is genuine warmth and gratitude
in their smiles and greetings. All of these small loyalty gestures engender big loyalty.

While formal programs can be a means to achieving loyalty, having
one is not a prerequisite. Big loyalty comes after customers have
interacted with your brand, received your marketing communications, tried your product, and experienced your customer service. The more you can make them feel special, the more loyalty

you will engender. What makes people feel special? Simple things like remembering what they've told you in the past and what their preferences are, and thanking them for their loyalty and patronage. As we've explored throughout this book, the united powers of the Geek, Nerd, and Suit are required to bring this to life.

Don't make the mistake of assuming that loyalty program membership is the same as customer loyalty itself. These programs can be a powerful component of a comprehensive strategy for making customers feel remembered, welcomed, and appreciated. But a points-for-purchases program alone does none of these things. Loyalty is actually a byproduct of a great customer experience. For some additional ideas for building big loyalty in your customers, read on.

Ⓖ Ⓝ Ⓢ DEFINE A CUSTOMER ENGAGEMENT SCORE

Loyalty program membership alone is not a measure of success! Even traditional customer satisfaction measures such as NPS or intent to purchase again may not be enough. A better measure of loyalty is a composite customer engagement score, which looks at all aspects of the customer experience and assigns a weighted score to each of the components that measurably impact the overall experience. While the best customer engagement score will be customized for each business, common components include: purchase frequency, marketing engagement rates, website/mobile app interactions, ratings and reviews, and customer satisfaction scores.

Ⓢ HAVE CUSTOMERS MAP THE CUSTOMER JOURNEY

While company employees may think they know all the steps in the customer journey, you need the customer's perspective on how they are feeling at each point along the way. Not only should you understand the sentiment or emotional impact of each touchpoint, but you should also understand the strength of that sentiment. Ultimately, you need to arrive at how important each of those journey points is to your customers, so you can prioritize where to invest in building engagement and loyalty over time. Invite some of your best customers to participate in this exercise. You may be surprised by how passionate they are, and how eye opening their perspectives prove to be.

❶ ❺ INSPIRE ASPIRATION

A tiered benefit structure for a loyalty program that rewards members more as they engage more with your brand can create an upwardly mobile customer base. Outside of the program, you can still identify promotions or perks that can appeal to your most valuable customers—whether they are in the program or not. The trick is to identify the aspirational goals of your customers, and position your product or service as a way to get there. Further, when you're thinking about what behaviors to reward, consider more than just how much they spend. If you want them engaged, make a game of it and challenge them to interact with you in new ways (e.g., download the mobile app, provide a product rating on your website, or refer a friend). This will make the program feel less tedious while building your customer relationships and expose customers to new options for interacting with you.

❻ ❶ ❺ DON'T PUNISH LOYALTY PROGRAM MEMBERS

Loyalty programs should make customer experience easier, not more complicated. However, many programs do the exact opposite, making it harder on customers if they're members—like by making them enter their email address every time they interact with you.

Programs that promise faster service times (e.g., Starbucks' order and pay in app), priority access (e.g., early access to sale pricing or private events), or higher levels of service (e.g., routing to a priority customer service line) make membership feel like a blessing, rather than a curse. Often, these "soft" benefits can be even more rewarding than the "hard" earned program benefits that anchor the program. Start by making loyalty membership the easiest way to do business with you, not the hardest.

ⓝ ⓢ KEEP BENEFITS SIMPLE

Although you may be tempted to wow your customers with a gigantic list of potential benefits that can be earned through customer loyalty, chances are they won't remember most of them. When we conduct loyalty research for our clients, they are almost always surprised at how abysmal benefit awareness is, even among their best customers and even for their stated "most important" benefit. Stick with fewer and more high-impact benefits and you're likely to see an improvement in benefit awareness, usage, and word-of-mouth. Add too many and you risk customers losing sight of even the most valuable of benefits amid a slew of irrelevant perks.

THE TAKEAWAY

There are a number of ways to generate loyalty, some of which leverage the construct of a formal loyalty program and some that don't. But customer engagement *can* be created without points, discounts, or gimmicks. How? By understanding the customer journey, creating a sense of aspiration, tracking the types of behaviors that truly tell you if customers are advocates for your brand, and by remembering the customer's interactions with you, using that information to make future interactions better. At its best, your loyalty program should be the easiest and best way for customers to experience your brand—especially for customers who are truly loyal.

LET'S FOCUS ON THESE 19 THINGS

If we told you that we have worked with a number of companies who have too many strategic priorities, you might end up stifling a yawn. Yes, we know this problem has been around since the beginning of strategic goal setting. Whether caused by a poorly articulated set of priorities that are "whispered down the lane" without oversight, or by a collaborative approach to goal-setting in which everyone can add their favorites to the list, this problem hasn't shown any signs of going away.

The challenge we're facing in business today is not the need to raise awareness of the existence of too many priorities—it's a challenge of prioritization. One leader we'll call Bryan once shared with us his company's 19 strategic priorities. Six were so huge that the retailer would be lucky to achieve just one of them in his lifetime. The other 13 were so tiny that conquering them would never make much of a difference for the business. What was puzzling, however, was that they were all presented as apparent equals to the organization, which left Bryan's team to their own devices. It was like a *Choose Your Own Adventure* novel—*The Cave of 19 Strategic Priorities.* The reality, as Bryan knew, was that a random, choose-your-own-adventure approach to resource distribution was going to be ineffective in driving meaningful change. So, what is the right way to prioritize?

We've all probably heard the rock-pebbles-sand analogy of prioritization by Dr. Stephen Covey: start by putting in the most important items (rocks), then add some medium-priority items (pebbles), and finally fill the gaps with the least important items (sand). This is a particularly helpful way to prioritize how to spend your limited amount of time in life, since it only requires you to look inward to determine what matters the most to you. Adding in a significant other to the mix complicates things a little, but again a compromise of mutual prioritization can usually be reached fairly easily. Plus, it allows you to delegate the priorities you'd rather avoid—such as paying the bills—to someone else.

In business, this approach isn't quite as straightforward as it sounds, because there is almost always debate about what the most important strategic business issues are. You can't really blame a business leader for looking at the business from their unique functional perspective (since it really is part of their job), but this naturally leads to very different adventures through *The Cave of 19 Strategic Priorities.* Sales teams will say the business needs more focus on customer acquisition, IT will tell you that a system upgrade is required, procurement will tell you that cost-reduction programs will drive success, and merchants will tell you that product innovation is the way to go.

Why is having too many top-level strategic priorities such a business impediment? Because it invariably creates confusion—both within an organization and out in the marketplace. Leaders and employees feel pulled in too many directions to do any one thing well. To handle the overload, they may decide to concentrate on the one or two priorities that they see as most relevant to their corner of the business or the easiest to address, at the expense of the rest. The result is a lack of coordination and alignment that radiates through every level of the organization. Worst of all, it can nearly always be felt by customers. If a hotel chain decided to run a special on weekend stays (for vacationers) at the same time it's running a weeknight promotion (for business travelers) at the same time it's running a partnership promotion with a regional airline, don't you think customers would be slightly confused? And don't get us started on measuring progress against all those objectives!

So how can a company shift from having a dozen sprawling objectives to just a few top priorities around which the entire company and all of its leaders are fully and happily aligned? The answer is simple: by putting customers and their needs at the center of that decision process. Customer perspective can become the objective point of view that is needed to end debates about prioritization. All of that insight you built in the customer foundation will tell you what matters most to your customers and your business.

In our experience, the common thread among companies bogged down by long lists of priorities is that somewhere in the process of deciding their top objectives, they become preoccupied with their own concerns and stop taking into consideration what their customers were already telling them through their words and their actions. The more objectives business leaders generate without using customer insight as a key filter, the more they can't seem to decide which objectives to keep and which ones to toss—so they keep them all.

When strategic priorities are tightly aligned to customer needs, they have a way of sorting themselves out more easily—with less debate and fewer personal agendas in the mix. The company we mentioned with 19 priorities? They turned to their customers and learned that they cared most about having a great mobile experience and having the ability to customize their preferences.

SAMPLE STRATEGIC PRIORITY LIST: BEFORE AND AFTER A CUSTOMER-CENTRIC FILTER

Priorities Before a Customer-Centric Filter	Priorities After a Customer-Centric Filter
1. Increase customer acquisition by 2%	1. Design master customer identification plan and build customer data warehouse
2. Upgrade email software	
3. Increase email conversion rates	
4. Launch new online checkout flow	2. Increase cross-channel purchase behavior and mobile app adoption
5. Build NPS dashboard	
6. Lower call center costs by 5%	3. Increase customer retention by improving product mix tailored to best customers
7. Increase customer identification	
8. Implement new hire rotation program	
9. Renegotiate agency agreements	
10. Grow bottom line profits by $10M	
11. Launch connected product with QR code marketing	
12. Restructure shared services organization	
13. Explore market expansion opportunities	
14. Update social sharing strategy	
15. Develop systematic traffic capture approach	
16. Connect web data to in-store transaction data	
17. Increase reactivation rates by 3%	
18. Expand loyalty program benefits	
19. Increase same store sales by 10%	

This shift is critical, because the "19 things" problem has a nasty habit of taking other forms. The impulse to generate and add rather than focus and distill can confuse an organization and all of its decisions. Trying to cram one more item into a product assortment, or a few more keywords onto a website, is really the "19 things" problem at a different scale. And, it can create an "anything goes" attitude that leads to some pretty un-strategic choices. Like a beverage company deciding to add diet cherry vanilla sour cream cinnamon soda to its product mix just because each of those products individually sold well (OK, maybe not the sour cream part), or a retailer deciding to sell thousand-dollar handbags even though its customer base liked buying bags (*from that very same brand!*) for a third of that.

When it comes to both strategic priorities and product offerings, less is almost always more. Unbounce co-founder Oli Gardner has been quoted as saying: "One page. One purpose. Period." A case study by *Marketing Sherpa* noted how Whirlpool increased its click-through rates more than 40 percent by simply reducing the number of calls-to-action. Apply these principles to marketing communications, and you get this: one primary message, or call to action, per communication.

Customers like simplification and convenience. The best way to find that focus is to start with customers themselves. Target Stores understood this when, in the 1990s, its leaders were pondering how to sell more laundry detergent. Instead of flinging a bunch of new brands onto the shelf, they looked carefully at what customers were buying—and it led them to do the opposite. They went from offering nine detergents to offering just six, based on the brands customers already preferred. What happened? Sales spiked. Removing products instead of adding more probably felt like a radical act, but focusing on the products customers cared about paid off.

For companies used to juggling tons of priorities, setting the organization's strategic course based in large part on consumer insight can feel revolutionary or even counterintuitive. But we've seen the results, again and again. Companies that do this are more focused, more responsive, and much more in touch with what their customers want and need.

So what should the Geek, the Nerd, and the Suit do to keep the company focused by focusing first on its customers?

❶ ❺ PRIORITIZE—TWICE!

If you have a list of possible strategic objectives, run it against what you already know about what your customers want and how they're behaving. Find out what your *customers* think your priorities should be. No matter how great it might sound to sell thousand-dollar handbags, if customers don't want them, going *haute couture* won't work. Of course, you don't want to prioritize based solely on what customers say they want. The second step is to look at your now-winnowed list and prioritize what remains based on potential business value. How many people could you target with that option, what is its potential, and how easy will it be for you to go after those dollars? If you're wondering whether to focus on growing loyalty or acquisition, this two-step process can help drive that answer.

❺ MAKE YOUR PRIORITIES CONCRETE AND UNDERSTANDABLE

A company's core priorities should be simple enough that everyone in the organization can rattle them off and understand what they mean for their part of the business. Clarity will ensure that everybody "gets" them so they don't feel compelled to interpret them based on their personal best interests. Vague, almost spiritual statements about what the company aims to achieve ("We will change the world through our products") sound noble, but aren't actionable. Similarly, tiny goals ("Reduce the time it takes to reorder misspelled embroidered items by one second") also don't work. And wording matters. They need to be universally understood, eliminating the risk of interpretation that reflects siloed best interests.

Ⓖ Ⓝ MAP STRATEGIC PRIORITIES TO A PERFORMANCE DASHBOARD

Everyone in an organization should know its strategic priorities— but they should also be able to see how the company is doing against those priorities. Creating a dashboard means giving everyone a view into how the organization's strategies are mapping against the choices and preferences of real buying customers—and tracking this over time. Keeping score enables people to see if their actions are working, and to correct course if they aren't.

Ⓖ Ⓢ MAKE IT HAPPEN AUTOMAGICALLY

Where you can, have your technology team automate the execution of some of your priorities so you don't have to think about them anymore. If one company priority is to begin sending a series of follow-on emails to every customer that makes a purchase, then make it automatic that the customers on that list get those messages every week, month, or at whatever cadence.

Ⓝ CREATE A "CUSTOMER 101"

In a high-performing culture, all of a company's leaders are serving the same customers. But they may spend most of their time focusing on such sliced and diced data about those customers that they lose their big-picture sense of who they are and what they've reported to the company about their experiences and their needs. Merchandising is looking at one view, while marketing is looking at another—and that influences the way they interpret the company's overall strategies. That's why it's so important for every leader in the organization to be operating with the same understanding of who they are serving. By offering a baseline grounding in customer insight to everyone, customer understanding can become more infused in the decisions made at every level of the organization. Just be sure to refresh that understanding regularly, so that leaders aren't aligning to a consistent, but outdated customer perspective.

⓪ USE CUSTOMER DATA TO REMOVE BIAS

Every executive has an opinion about where the business should be heading that may be more or less grounded in experience and fact. One exec thinks one thing, one thinks another. When they're all looking at aggregated consumer insights, it's not uncommon for them to lean on existing data that supports their personal bias. This is where the customer foundation (introduced in Chapter 12) can again come into play. Customer analytics designed to answer a specific strategic question should help eliminate these interpersonal conflicts and provide an answer that gets everybody back on common ground.

THE TAKEAWAY

Having too many top-level strategic priorities can stand in the way of a company's progress (not to mention its profits) by creating confusion and lack of focus at every level of the organization. The key to narrowing down a long list of objectives to the best possible few is to bring customers and their needs into the conversation— while also remembering that less is almost always more. The customer perspective can be represented in a number of ways, from survey feedback to behavioral analytics, and it can typically shine a light on the elements of the business that are most important to customers. Further, because customer perspective can be tied to customer value, you'll end up with a built-in mechanism to estimate the potential opportunity from pursuing each potential business priority—taking the guesswork out of prioritization.

20

OSCAR DIGGS

We made a promise to one another that we would never share what we are about to share. It's one of those poignant details that we developed together as a kind of secret inside joke—one that started off as something silly, but eventually defined an archetype for a part of our job and our business that we find aggravating.

Oscar Diggs. There, we said it.

If you don't recognize the name, you'll recognize the pattern. We say it when we come across business leaders who are authoritarian crisis creators. You know the type. They are disrupters, but in the worst sense of the term. They create anxiety throughout the company because they seem to thrive on it and enjoy the drama, managing somehow to swoop in at the last minute and appear to be the heroes of their own catastrophes. They work like hell, often seem angry, and thrive on the fear they instill among others. Lacking trust in their employees and teams, and rarely listening to their customers, they are great and terrible kings to be feared. These are the Wizards of Oz.

So, who is this Diggs character? Oscar Diggs is the Wizard of Oz's name in L. Frank Baum's famous novel. And in the book, what did all that power and trickery and drama get Diggs? It got him anxiety, long hours in his curtained cubicle, loneliness, and failure. If it's being a feared dictator that you're after, the ideas in this book will not help you achieve it. And let's be honest for a second, more than a handful of figures in business today seem out to become versions of Oscar Diggs.

Many of the challenges we talked about in this book won't be accomplished by any one individual or the mythologized superhero executive. Even the most deified leaders—Chouinard, Jobs, Musk—achieved their triumphs through collaboration. They are all credited with building famous brands, products, and experiences, but the secret formula for their success involved giving up some control to empower the right people in the right way who take very seriously the challenge of listening, understanding, and responding to the customer. Solving these types of macro business problems requires partnership at every level.

Likewise, businesses themselves often fall into "Oscar Diggs Syndrome," deluding themselves into believing they have all of the power.

Wrong.

The customers have the power, and they prove it every day when they walk through your doors to shop, browse your website, and ultimately open their wallets. Their alternatives are vast and continue to grow, and the ways and places they choose to interact with a brand, product, or service are now all on their terms. The best we can do is listen to them, understand them, and take appropriate action. In gaming lingo, the customer is the house, and all companies will need to start stacking the deck in their favor by employing the principles in this book if they don't want to lose.

The beauty of the Geek + Nerd + Suit formula is that it can radically simplify decision-making across your business and, when done correctly, the "right answer" becomes self-evident and the business begins to run itself. It's not hard to get things to happen when Geeks, Nerds, and Suits are in the room together trying to solve the problem. It's even easier when they're all looking at the same customer truths to influence what they're doing.

As you move forward, keep a keen eye out for Oscar Diggs, knowing he can easily become the default. Diggs is the result of hackneyed business mythology and the entropy caused by big egos. Think of the Geek + Nerd + Suit partnership as the equalizer—the democratic glue that will not only hold a company together, but also create innovation and success beyond the mere hopes and dreams of its leaders. And if that sounds like hopeless optimism to you, just remember Yvon Chouinard taking five-month vacations as Patagonia thrived.

The hardest part of Geek + Nerd + Suit is trusting the model, trusting the teams, and trusting each other. But it's through that trust that the emergence occurs. Oscar Diggs persists in the belief that he can cut his own path to innovation, but we believe the path forward will always be clear if you use customer insight as your guide. If you think this book is about solving business problems, you're only half right. If you think this book is about working longer hours, think again. It's actually about working less, and doing more. It's about trusting that through the Geek + Nerd + Suit formula you will not only solve your problems, but also discover and create your next big breakthrough.

We have seen it happen. Our business is about making it happen. And we hope you will make it happen now, too.

For more information about *Geek Nerd Suit* or to take both our Customer Centricity Pain Point Quiz and our *Geek Nerd Suit* Personality Quiz, please visit www.geeknerdsuit.com.

ABOUT THE AUTHORS

CHUCK DENSINGER

As Elicit's COO, Chuck brings 25+ years of global retail, technology, and marketing experience. He is a seasoned executive who has spent his career helping Fortune 500 companies with technology- and analytics-based customer strategy, and has seen firsthand the success that comes from structuring business around the customer. Chuck is a University of Minnesota MBA and resides in Minnesota with his wife, Vicki. In his free time, he enjoys cooking, snowboarding, spending time with his two adult children, and is an avid Star Wars fan.

BROOKE NIEMIEC

Brooke is Elicit's CMO and has represented the voice of the customer for Fortune 100 companies (including Boeing, Disney, and JCPenney) for most of her 18-year career. She earned her MBA at the University of Southern California, and is an avid people watcher and question asker. Brooke has been published in Fast Company, CMO.com, and CRM Magazine, and was recently named a member of the Direct Marketing News Hall of Femme. A native Southern Californian, Brooke lives in Los Angeles with her husband, Jim and their two daughters.

MASON THELEN

Mason is Elicit's CEO and has a history of challenging the status quo, cultivating talent, and driving teams to innovate. Recent accolades include being named an Ernst & Young Entrepreneur of the Year Finalist and one of the 40 most influential marketers under 40 in America by Direct Marketing News. He's co-led IBM's advanced customer analytics practice, built loyalty programs for industry giants, and is the go-to-guy for many Fortune 500 executives. He's also a member of the Forbes Agency Council. A passionate outdoorsman, Mason lives in Minnesota with his wife, Danielle.

REFERENCES

OPENING: THE DIRTBAG

...**San Blas, Mexico...** Yvon Chouinard, *Let my People Go Surfing* (New York, NY: Penguin Books, 2005, 2006), 14

Inspired by a Swedenborgian mystic... "**By the early 1970s ...**" "**Through the 1980s...**" Patagonia website. "Company History." http://www.patagonia.com/company-history.html (accessed March 20, 2017).

"**There are two kinds of growth...**" "**We were growing too fast.**" Guy Raz, *How I Built This* (NPR, December 12, 2016). See: http://www.npr.org/podcasts/510313/how-i-built-this (accessed March 21, 2017).

"**At all levels...**" Yvon Chouinard, *Let my People Go Surfing*, 73.

"**If the warehouse burns down...**" "**A lot of companies are top-down management...**" Guy Raz, *How I Built This*.

CHAPTER 9

Southwest has managed to make a profit for over forty consecutive years. Ulfberht Capital, "Southwest Airlines: 40 Consecutive Years of Profit." (*Seeking Alpha*. April 1, 2013). https://seekingalpha.com/article/1312991-southwest-airlines-40-consecutive-years-of-profits (accessed April 6, 2017).

CHAPTER 18

...**Bain & Company found...** "Zero Defections: Quality Comes to Services" (Harvard Business Review, September-October 1990 Issue). https://hbr.org/1990/09/zero-defections-quality-comes-to-services (accessed May 20, 2017).

CHAPTER 19

Unbounce co-founder Oli Gardner… "Is Too Much Choice Killing Your Conversion Rates? [Case Studies]." (*Unbounce*. April 10, 2014). https://unbounce.com/conversion-rate-optimization/psychology-of-choice-conversion-rates/ (accessed April 10, 2017).

A case study by Marketing Sherpa… "Email Marketing: Whirlpool lifts clickthrough rate 42%, creates testing culture." (Marketing Sherpa. February 6, 2014). https://www.marketingsherpa.com/article/case-study/whirlpool-lift-clickthrough-testing-culture (accessed April 10, 2017).

CPSIA information can be obtained
at www.ICGtesting.com
Printed in the USA
FSOW04n0845100617
34961FS